Internal Landscapes and Foreign Bodies

Tavistock Clinic Series
Nick Temple, Margot Waddell (Series Editors)
Published and distributed by Karnac Books

Other titles in the Tavistock Clinic Series:

Assessment in Child Psychotherapy
Margaret Rustin and Emanuela Quagliata (editors)

Facing It Out: Clinical Perspectives on Adolescent Disturbance
Robin Anderson and Anna Dartington (editors)

Inside Lives: Psychoanalysis and the Growth of the Personality
Margot Waddell

Mirror to Nature: Drama, Psychoanalysis and Society
Margaret Rustin and Michael Rustin

Multiple Voices: Narrative in Systemic Family Psychotherapy
Renos K. Papadopoulos and John Byng-Hall (editors)

Psychoanalysis and Culture: A Kleinian Perspective
David Bell (editor)

Psychotic States in Children
Margaret Rustin, Maria Rhode, Alex Dubisky,
Hélène Dubinsky (editors)

Reason and Passion: A Celebration of the Work of Hanna Segal
David Bell (editor)

Surviving Space: Papers on Infant Observation
Andrew Briggs (editor)

Therapeutic Care for Refugees: No Place Like Home
Renos K. Papadopoulos (editor)

Understanding Trauma: A Psychoanalytic Approach
Caroline Garland (editor)

Orders
Tel: +44 (0)20 8969 4454; Fax: +44 (0)20 8969 5585
Email: shop@karnacbooks.com
www.karnacbooks.com

Internal Landscapes
and
Foreign Bodies

Eating Disorders and Other Pathologies

Gianna Williams

KARNAC

LONDON   NEW YORK

First published in 1997 by Gerald Duckworth & Co. Ltd.
Second impression 2000
This edition printed in 2002 by
H. Karnac (Books) Ltd
6 Pembroke Buildings, London NW10 6RE
Tel. +44 (0)20 8969 4454
Fax. +44 (0)20 8969 5585
A subsidiary of Other Press LLC, New York

A catalogue record for this book is available
from the British Library

ISBN 1 85575 972 1

Edition amendments by The Studio Publishing Services Ltd,
Exeter EX4 8JN

Printed in Great Britain

Contents

For Martha Harris
In Memory

Series Editors' Preface

Since it was founded in 1920, the Tavistock Clinic has developed a wide range of therapeutic approaches to mental health which have been strongly influenced by the ideas of psychoanalysis. It has also adopted systemic family therapy as a theoretical model and a clinical approach to family problems. The Clinic is now the largest training institution in Britain for mental health, providing postgraduate and qualifying courses in social work, psychology, psychiatry, anbd child, adolcescent, and adult psychotherapy, as well as in nursing and primary care. It trains about 1,400 students each year in over 45 courses.

The Clinic's philosophy aims at promoting therapeutic methods in mental health. Its work is founded on the clinical expertise that is also the basis of its consultancy and research activities. The aim of this Series is to make available to the reading public the clinical, theoretical, and research work that is most influential at the Tavistock Clinic. The Series sets out new approaches in the understanding and treatment of psychological disturbance in children, adolescents, and adults, both as individuals and in families.

Internal Landscapes and Foreign Bodies explores the problems which arise in forming and sustaining intimate relationships. This book is based on Gianna Williams's work over many years in the Tavistock Clinic, including work in the Eating Disorders Workshop of the Adolescent Department. It examines how dependency is defended against in a variety of ways which involve refusing to take in good experiences, by keeping some relationships at bay and controlling others. These defences can take the form of eating disorders but also have an important significance in a variety of other pathologies. Gianna Williams provides a subtle understanding of some of the obstacles which stand in the way of patients seeking and receiving therapeutic help.

Nicholas Temple and Margot Waddell
Series Editors

Acknowledgements

I have been helped very generously by a number of friends with the work on this book. I wish to mention particularly Simonetta Adamo, Vera Forster, Cathy Urwin, Paul Williams and Margot Waddell. Ann Scott has been invaluable in her highly professional editing of the manuscript, and Lyndsay MacDonald indefatigable in the endless typing and supportive with her friendly, cheerful availability.

I am grateful to Donald Meltzer for helping me to develop an intense interest in 'internal landscapes'. I wish also to express gratitude to a number of supervisors who helped me with some of the cases quoted in the book: amongst them are Esther Bick, Irma Brenman Pick, Martha Harris, Roger Money-Kyrle, Frances Tustin and Isca Wittenberg. Many thanks to the students and colleagues who have allowed me to quote material from their observations or clinical work, amongst them Miranda Davies, Jane Ellwood, Marta Martin, Bianca Micanzi-Ravagli and Mariangela Pinheiro.

I wish to thank Elizabeth Bott Spillius for the very significant help she gave me in finding space in my mind for this book. Last but not least I would like to thank my husband, Arthur, for his support and co-operation, my mother, Maria Bianca, my daughters Sue and Claudia and my grand-daughter Chiara, for their appropriate and often helpful impatience with my inordinate devotion to work.

Author's Note

This book consists of a number of papers written at different times. I selected them following a thread I have highlighted in the Introduction.

The drawing on the cover is by a five-and-a-half-year-old boy suffering from feeding difficulties and exhibiting some autistic features.

Introduction

The central theme of the book is impairment in 'taking from another' in internalising a dependent relationship. This impairment manifests itself at times in the context of the psychopathology of eating disorders. The relationship between difficulties in taking in within the context of dependent relationships and the concreteness of problems with food intake has interested me over many years.

The first chapter of the book – The Inner World of the Child – was presented at a conference to a large and varied audience. In this particular chapter I focus almost exclusively on the nature of the internal landscape of the child. The patient described, Louise, a young adolescent, had developed defences against forming a dependent relationship which could not be seen as a consequence of traumatic experience, nor of deprivation either in her early history or her current life. I describe in this chapter the nature of some unholy internal alliances which help the patient to maintain the status quo offering her protection from the pain associated with dependent relationships. In this case the unholy alliances are not of the magnitude of the 'pathological organisations' (Steiner, 1982; 1987) I will refer to when talking about other patients later in the book.

The second chapter, Thinking and Learning in Deprived Children, considers the predicament of patients who have been deprived of the experience of a container and whose equipment for thinking and learning is impaired as a consequence. This chapter is in marked contrast with the first one as it highlights *external* deprivation as a central factor. I rely heavily on the frame of reference supplied by Wilfred Bion in his theory of 'container/contained' (Bion, 1962). Bion suggests that the equipment necessary for giving a name to emotional experiences and making them thinkable is the internalisation of an external object capable of performing such a function, i.e. the 'container'. I was intrigued to find in a paper I wrote in 1968 (Henry [Williams], 1969) how an unusually verbal seven-year-old girl seemed to have a notion of the function of a containing object at a time when I had not as yet become properly acquainted with the theory of container/ contained and the parallel offered by Bion between physiological and psychic digestion. Seven-year-old Sarah told me: 'My digestive system is not very good, you digest the food for me in your stomach and give me back what goes into my bloodstream' (Henry [Williams], 1969, p. 55). Sarah's statement that her 'digestive system is not very good' is echoed in Chapter 2 in several examples of the predicament of children with a faulty psychic apparatus, who need to internalise the function of an object capable of making emotional sense of their experiences. I also address in this chapter the question of experiences which are so traumatic (where the external input is experienced as psychologically so intolerable) that even well-endowed children, including those who have not been previously traumatised, would probably find them indigestible and unable to be absorbed into their emotional 'bloodstream'. I therefore draw attention to both *faulty equipment* and *intolerable input*.

Chapter 3, Double Deprivation, describes certain aspects of the treatment of a patient who had developed highly impervious defences to ward off the experience of need and dependency. This particular patient, Martin, was far more resistant than the majority of patients I have encountered: external factors undoubtedly greatly contributed to the construction of his edifice of defences against object dependency. Traumatic experiences and severe deprivation were present in his early years.

So far, it can be seen that I have addressed first of all the discrepancy between the nature of external experiences and the quality of the internal world (in Chapter 1) and subsequently, the impact of external experiences on the quality of internalisation and of the texture of the internal landscape (Chapter 2). There might be said to be almost a polarisation between the first two chapters. This I attempt to bridge in Chapter 3. The work I describe with my patient Martin has permitted me to reflect on the relative contribution of internal and external factors to the nature of the internal landscape. Martin had protected himself from feelings of dependency and the need of another (as had Louise in Chapter 1) but in his case the development of his defences can be seen to be closely related to a protection against psychic pain which might have been unbearable at an extremely early stage in his life. The title Double Deprivation refers to the dispossession inflicted by external factors, but also to the loss engendered by the development of defences which made this patient an orphan inwardly, not merely outwardly.

In Chapters 4 and 5 I move on to consider the types of internal alliance which offer protection from the psychic pain associated with dependent relationships. In Chapter 4, On Gang Dynamics, the narcissistic personality structure of the patient described clearly provides an *addictive* as opposed to a *dependent* relationship. This question of internal unholy alliances is further considered in Chapter 5, Self-Esteem and Object Esteem, but the clinical material cited here does not show evidence of such a deeply entrenched 'pathological organisation' (Steiner, 1993), but more a type of chronic addiction to denigration of the object, which makes dependency on such an object particularly unattractive. The title of Chapter 5 refers to the ways in which the denigration of the object falls like a shadow on the patient's perception of herself (Freud, 1917).

On the Process of Internalisation (Chapter 6) describes the process of the gradual internalisation of an object which is sufficiently reliable to make dependency possible. The patient I talk about was probably more traumatised than any of the patients presented elsewhere in the book. I return here to the theme of the first chapter in so far as I describe a clinical case where there appears to be *no linear cause and effect between external traumatic factors and the magnitude of the patient's defences*. The patient in question was severely deprived, as well as born with a serious physical disability. In spite of that he had not retreated into a 'pathological organisation', nor had he developed impervious defences against dependency (like those of Martin in Chapter 3). Omnipotent defences loomed large, but here they seemed to perform the survival function of primitive omnipotence as described by Joan Symington (1983).

The final five chapters of the book touch upon a range of feeding difficulties or eating disorders which may be seen as further facets of the pathology associated with impairments in 'taking from another'. For example, Chapter 7, Poor Feeders, presents examples of this phenomenon, beginning with an infant who refused to be fed from the day he was born and only very gradually accepted nourishment. Additional examples are provided from a range of settings in which the dynamics of resistance against dependency are clearly apparent: this resistance can appear in the context of learning, or the context of experiencing missing and pining and acknowledging the pain of separation.

In Chapter 8, Reversal of the 'Container/Contained' Relationship, I have come to develop a number of ideas on the theme of the use of children as recipients of projections. Since I wrote this particular chapter I have reached the conclusion that in circumstances where children are at the receiving end of projections, the terms container and contained should not be merely reversed, but rather 'container' should be replaced with 'receptacle' and 'contained' with 'foreign body'.

Some of the material I describe in Chapter 9, The No-Entry System of Defences, provides a retrospective, probably deeper, understanding of the case of a psychotic girl whom I had in analysis over twenty years ago (cf. Chapter 8) in the light of material which emerged in the therapy of a seventeen year old I treated in recent years. In both cases the fear, or even dread, of something inimical 'coming inside' is experienced very concretely. In the seventeen-year-old anorexic patient this occurred in dream form in nightmares where all orifices of her body were invaded by tadpoles. In the psychotic girl I treated twenty years ago there occurred a concrete delusion of fleas penetrating every orifice. Both patients suffered from severe eating disorders, and now I think that in both cases one of the contributory factors to the psychopathology was an early experience of having been a receptacle for parental projections.

My interest has centred in recent years on this particular contributory factor to eating disorders. Some patients protect themselves from the experience of an inimical input and develop what I have described as a no-entry system of defences. These patients are more frequently anorexic than bulimic.

In Chapters 10 and 11 I turn my attention to the experience of patients who remain 'porous' to parental projections. Their symptomatology, in the context of eating disorders, manifests itself predominantly as bulimia. The title of Chapter 10 On Introjective Processes refers to the formulation of a hypothesis based on Wilfred Bion's theory of an organising function in the internal world that he calls 'alpha function'. I suggested that patients who have introjected an object overflowing with projections, may also internalise a *function* which is the obverse of alpha function, a disorganising one which could be called 'omega function'.

In Chapter 11, Foreign Bodies, I continue to deal with the theme of eating disorders as being intimately connected with a difficulty in 'taking from another' and as a defence against the psychic pain experienced when a dependent relationship with a unique, precious and irreplaceable object is established. The bulimic patient I describe in this chapter experienced himself as invaded by foreign bodies akin to the fleas of Natasha in Chapter 8, and of the tadpoles of Sally in Chapter 9. He had indeed been at the receiving end of massive projections from a very disturbed mother. His difficulty in taking in was partly associated with the fear of being invaded by this type of foreign body.

The chapter is mainly centred on material that emerged in the fourth year of this patient's analysis when he was attending four times a week. It became increasingly clear that attention to the persecutory nature of foreign bodies, seen as a consequence of parental projections, could distract the analytic work from attention to an alternative meaning of foreign bodies, namely the painful Oedipal experience of the presence of a 'third one' in the transference relationship. The presence of a paternal function is essential for a dependent relationship on the maternal object to become established, but is often perceived as inimical (Britton, 1989).

I wrote Chapter 11 with the aim of drawing together some of the themes that run through the previous chapters. The spasmodic need to control food intake which is present both in anorexia and bulimia can be associated at times with a fear of being invaded by something inimical, but it also serves the function of avoiding dependency on relationships that are not so easy to control, that are not always available. One can see that the shift from the control of food in my patient Daniel was still present in in his voracious relationship to literature. Although less dangerous than the eating disorder symptom, the meaning of needing to control an object which he never needed to wait for continued to be present for a long time. It is relevant here that he had been in an incubator for the first weeks of his life. Experiences do not need to be so traumatic for a child to develop a controlling relationship to his objects; for instance 'teddy-bear' parents in Chapter 1 or a robot, with or without a battery, in Chapter 2 are still within the realm of relationship to things (objects) devoid of any life and freedom of their own. In the later development of Daniel's analysis, one can observe his gradual relinquishing of a spasmodic control over inanimate objects such as food and of his control of human relationships, and a shift to the dangerous ground of dependent object relationships. Such relationships, viz. the one developed with me in the transference, are unique and irreplaceable while a bar of chocolate is just like another, and, at the time of voracious reading, a book was also for Daniel just like another. I think it becomes clear in this chapter that the relinquishment of defences against forming a dependent relationship with a human being, free to come and go, of which we have seen many different examples throughout the book, represents a shift especially in the area of eating disorders, from valuing possessions to valuing a different aspect in one's quality of life. It could probably be most concisely defined as a transition from lending value to *having*, to finding greater fulfilment in the more painful but richer predicament of *being*.

1
The Inner World of the Child

In attempting to describe the model I have in mind when I refer to the Inner World of the Child, I will not start with a definition, but with a vivid recollection of an exhibition of children's paintings which was for me a significant experience. The paintings had a common theme, since the village where the children lived had recently been flooded by a river running through it. The flood had not been great, and no human lives were lost. The very perceptive head teacher of the village school suggested that the children make a picture of what had happened on the day of the flood. It was striking that although the children had shared the same experience – no part of the village had been more affected by the flood than another – the paintings varied enormously.

I remember that one of them showed the village completely covered with water so that only the bell-tower could be seen; a number of people were portrayed on top of the bell-tower, which had a flat roof, and some had a very frightened expression. The picture also showed a shark and a sword-fish floating in the water, both of them highly unlikely creatures to inhabit a river. I also vividly remember another picture – a little boy and a man, who I guessed was his father, were carrying sacks up the half-flooded stairs from a flooded cellar, and the sacks were realistically marked as containing food provisions. Other paintings were extremely vivid in colour, and I remember an abundance of red Wellington boots. Probably the most cheerful pictures made me feel uncomfortable because I doubted that this experience could have been a purely amusing one, like a good opportunity for a paddle. But I was certainly struck by the variety of the paintings, and it gave me an opportunity to see how varied children's reactions to the same external experience can be.

In terms of the internal world, I would like to suggest that at least one of the reasons why the same experience was portrayed in such different ways by different children was that it was filtered through an internal frame of reference: I would take the varied representations of the flood to be a reflection of differences in the children's inner reality.

When we attempt to understand the origin of such differences it is difficult to make a clear-cut separation of the elements deriving from nature, and the elements deriving from nurture, in the making of the inner world.

The aspect of the inner world, then, that I would particularly like to focus on in this chapter is the subjective element that influences and colours the perception of external events. I am going to describe aspects of my work with a patient that may help to illustrate more clearly what I refer to when talking about the inner world. I have deliberately chosen a case whose external circumstances were *not* particularly traumatic, as this might help one to focus on the subjective component of the inner world, rather than look for external causes. In the case of my patient, a girl chronologically in her teens but emotionally in her early childhood, the reason for disturbance could not be very clearly pinpointed in terms of her history. Yet, though the cause was uncertain, its effects were undeniable.

The Cheshire Cat

Louise was referred to the clinic by her school, where she was described as being switched-off and out of touch. She had no friends, and the teachers found it difficult to establish contact with her. Her actual school work did not seem to be greatly affected. Louise was very imaginative in her essays, but they were said to be at times 'a little weird'. She was able to learn, but related much better to books than to people. There were some aloof features in her which engendered concern about the possibility of a deterioration, and of her drifting even further away from relationships as she got further into adolescence. Nobody knew of any traumatic experiences in Louise's childhood except for a separation of two weeks from her parents when she was three and a half. A year later, a little brother was born and Louise found it hard to adjust to the birth of this child. Her father had taken time off from work and looked after her while Mother was in hospital.

When I first saw Louise, I was struck by her very young appearance. Although she was tall for her age, she really looked much more like a twelve year old than a fourteen year old – very thin, rather lanky – and her large dark eyes didn't focus on me when I first met her. In fact, the difficulty in meeting her eyes was one of the aspects that most struck me on that occasion.

I will start by describing some instances from my early work with her. On occasions when Louise was sitting in an armchair facing me, talking and apparently in touch, a cloud would form between us. She could no longer be reached, and it seemed that her mind had wandered away. This happened a number of times. At first, I thought she might have switched off as a defence, in order to avoid something painful that had emerged at that moment; but her attention seemed to fade away just as easily and suddenly at other times, when it seemed unlikely that this could be the case. I was often taken by surprise by her.

I then began to think that her behaviour might have a different meaning and unconscious purpose. Perhaps what really mattered was Louise's need *for me* to experience the feelings evoked by her sudden 'disappearances'. Indeed, I often did feel very lost: I did not know where she was, whether she could actually hear what I was saying. In addition to that, I was at times puzzled by a strange smile, and a sort of grin that came over Louise's face and contrasted with her blank expression. I wondered whether Louise might not have a need to evoke in me a painful feeling that she herself could not bear – perhaps the only way she could tell me about it.

Sometimes, she scribbled during her sessions. On one occasion, she got engrossed in drawing, producing a picture very similar to the face of the Cheshire Cat. She said it looked like an illustration in her copy of *Alice in Wonderland* (a book she was particularly fond of). It was a picture of the cat's face with a very wide grin on it amidst the foliage of a tree. At first, she talked about the cat's features as if they were something attractive: she liked the cat's elusiveness and its mockery, features to which I had to some extent been exposed in my relationship with her. I tried to put this to Louise as simply as I could, saying that at times she had behaved with me in a very elusive and slippery 'Cheshire Cat' sort of way, and that there was even sometimes a sort of smile on her face which seemed to fit in with that picture. Perhaps, I said, she wished me to have an experience like Alice's with the cat: we could try to understand together what this might be about.

I shall not describe in detail the process involved in sharing with Louise the perception of the slippery, elusive quality she sometimes put across. I often told her that she wished me to feel something I knew she could not as yet convey verbally: she wished me to know how it felt to be with someone and not really know how long that person was going to be available, present and giving of attention. I thought – and still think – that Louise needed *me* to feel this uncertainty and the anxiety that went with it, in order to convey the quality of a crucial aspect of her inner world, one crucial to her feeling so adrift in life. If the central character of her inner world was a Cheshire Cat type of object, elusive and extremely unreliable with an element of mockery or cruelty, it was not surprising that she had very little to hold on to in order to cope with anxiety. Indeed, such an object would not protect her from anxiety, but engender it.

An important part of my work with Louise consisted in providing her with an experience of attention and consistency, which gradually began to counterbalance the elusive quality of the Cheshire Cat, there one minute and gone the next. It is hard to know how this image developed within Louise's mind. From what we know of her mother, we might wonder if she had been able to devote enough attention to her child, but I do not think there is any basis for thinking that Louise was ever treated with deliberate cruelty. On the other hand, she probably *felt* treated with cruelty, most of all when her younger sibling was born.

As I have said, there was a period of months during treatment when Louise *herself* was the Cheshire Cat, and I was confronted with the 'disappearances' and the 'grin', together with the feelings that they evoked in me. Some changes then started to take place. Louise became much less elusive and very gradually more able to confront the pain she had avoided by being the Cheshire Cat. The less she herself was the Cheshire Cat with me, the more she began to perceive *me* as elusive and unpredictable. I remember her insisting on one occasion, for example, that I had stopped in mid-sentence, as if *my* mind had wandered off. In fact, I had ended a sentence with a question mark that Louise had not heard in the tone of my voice. There were instances of distortion that we could observe together during the sessions, but mostly I became the Cheshire Cat for her when the sessions ended. Any 'good-bye', even that at the end of a session, was perceived as a cruel disappearance, almost as if I were laughing at a small child for making such a fuss about being abandoned. The way she experienced me appeared to be filtered through the image of an internal Cheshire Cat-like mother.

It was important to prepare Louise very carefully for holidays, and even to talk about the approaching end of a particular session, letting her know that there were only five minutes to go. She could not tolerate abrupt 'disappearances'. On one occasion, when there was good contact between us, Louise referred to Alice's plea to the Cheshire Cat, please, to disappear more slowly. Consistent drawing of Louise's attention to this aspect of her inner world, and comparing it with outer reality, brought about further *gradual* modifications; she came to relate to an inner image that was a little more reliable and less cruel than the Cheshire Cat. It was a long process, and I am now going to try and describe some of its stages in more detail.

Teddy-Bear Parents

The gradual modifications were, I think, more the consequence of the texture of the relationship that developed between us than related to the *content* of my interpretations. As I said earlier, an important part of my work with Louise consisted in providing her with an *experience* of attention and consistency. Louise needed to feel sufficiently contained to be able to relinquish the protection of harmful defences and face the psychic pain that had previously been intolerable. In her case, the intolerable pain was the perception of a slippery, elusive, unreliable quality, most probably derived from her perception of her mother. Her harmful defence was to reverse the situation and become elusive, unreachable and out of touch herself.

A great deal of anxiety was in store for her once she began to be more in touch with her feelings and phantasies about *my* not being constantly available.[1] Gradually Louise began to trust me to be there at the expected time, and not to suddenly disappear. A differentiation slowly developed between the teenager who could make do with some degree of uncertainty and the younger child in her, who expected me to be available on demand. For the younger child, my freedom to come and go was quite intolerable. I was also supposed to be quite unchangeable in my appearance: Louise could be very disturbed by my wearing a dress she had never seen before, and even more by a change of hairstyle.

She had memories of her teddy bears, a collection of them, when she was a little girl, and she still kept two of them. It became evident that she would have preferred me to be like her teddy bears: teddy-bear parents remain where you leave them, they don't have a life of their own. This image can be seen to represent a change in Louise's inner world, from an elusive and unpredictable Cheshire Cat to a deadly teddy-bear type of couple. But neither the cat nor the teddy-bear parents could provide her with much help or firm holding.

A rather extreme example of deadening control over parent figures comes to mind from another treatment. A little boy, who used to bring a robot with a battery to his sessions, clutched the battery with one hand and the robot with the other. It was *extremely* important that the battery be left outside the robot so that it wouldn't move. At times, he brought the robot and left the battery at home. One might say that a robot with

[1] A clear picture of what is meant by 'always available' was provided by a little girl patient of mine who could go to sleep only if the tap in the kitchen, which was off her room, was left running. For her this meant that supplies were forever flowing.

a battery is not the most caring of parent images anyhow, but a robot without a battery is deprived of all movement and life. At this stage, the patient was himself a very lifeless little boy. There was no battery or heart in his inner world.

The teddy-bear parents couldn't provide much life for Louise either. Certainly, they could not be of much avail in helping her to use her potentialities. For instance, they could not provide an inspiring identification for her sexual development.

It must be evident by now how far Louise was from her chronological age, and how little she had touched on adolescence. However, a change *had* taken place in her external relationships, for by this time she was much less withdrawn. She had made some friends in school: they were girl friends only, although the school was mixed, but this was a step forward. She was no longer relating exclusively to books. She might also have had some helpful friends, but I never heard about them at this point. I heard only about the anti-treatment 'friends'.

'Proper Assistance'

It may well be understandable why Louise so much needed to find within herself and externally allies who would protect her from missing and valuing me. It was probably just because the relationship with me was becoming more important to her, and hence my absences more painful, that she became very sensitive to the opinions of her 'friends'. Apparently, news of where she was going when she left lessons to come for treatment had spread, and she reported that in school *'they'* were 'making fun' of her. This may have been true, but knowing how easily Louise could find a Cheshire Cat sort of mockery when there wasn't any, I was not quite certain. I did not know whether the school friends were really helping her in her anti-treatment campaign. It appeared to me that, whatever her friends said, she was very welcoming of a voice that told her 'Don't go there – it is really no good for you'. This was probably an *internal* voice saying that change could be less painful – and what about no change at all?

After a period of uphill sessions, in which I tried to draw Louise's attention to this *internal* voice that matched the reported external voices, on one occasion she made a co-operative response. She said I had reminded her of a dialogue in *Alice in Wonderland* – no, it was in *Through the Looking-Glass* – and she paraphrased the dialogue. As, unlike Louise, I do not know the book by heart, I shall quote from the actual text. What follows is the exchange between Humpty Dumpty and Alice on the subject of her age:

> '... So here's a question for you. How old did you say you were?'
> Alice made a short calculation and said 'Seven years and six months'.
> 'Wrong!' Humpty Dumpty exclaimed triumphantly. 'You never said a word like it.'
> 'I thought you meant "How old *are* you?" ' Alice explained.
> 'If I'd meant that, I'd have said it,' said Humpty Dumpty.
> Alice didn't want to begin another argument, so she said nothing.
> 'Seven years and six months!' Humpty Dumpty repeated thoughtfully. 'An uncomfortable sort of age. Now if you'd asked my advice, I'd have said "Leave it off at seven" – but it's too late now.'
> 'I never ask advice about growing,' Alice said indignantly.
> 'Too proud?' the other enquired.
> Alice felt even more indignant at this suggestion. 'I mean,' she said, 'that one can't help growing older.'
> '*One* [my italics] can't, perhaps,' said Humpty Dumpty, 'but *two* [my italics] can. With proper assistance, you might have left off at seven.' (1872, pp. 271-2)

This association to the dialogue between Alice and Humpty Dumpty was, I felt, a turning-point in my work with Louise. She appeared to be saying that the anti-treatment voices came from a somewhat doubtful source – the source of 'proper assistance' that can bring growth and development to a standstill.

At this stage, Louise appeared to be more open to work with me in identifying the *internal* obstacle, the (actually) improper assistance that had stunted her development. She could begin to see that perhaps it wasn't solely the responsibility of an elusive, unpredictable mother. (Certainly, by this time, I was not perceived as so unreliable.) Nor was it perhaps the fault of parents who would not settle for a teddy-bear status, for being controlled, and who reserved for themselves the freedom to come and go, to have other children. Louise was very aware of not being my one and only patient. This had been a great source of grievance during the most controlling phase of her treatment. But now that the grievances were beginning to lessen, she was becoming increasingly interested in understanding what Humpty Dumpty could stand for within herself.

Some of Louise's associations appeared quite meaningful in this respect. She remembered that Humpty Dumpty, perched on his high wall, said to Alice that there was no chance of his falling off; but she said that this didn't match the nursery rhyme, in which he *did* fall and 'all the king's horses and all the king's men couldn't put Humpty together again'. It looked as if she was beginning to feel able to relinquish some of the omnipotence of her defences. Louise also said that Humpty Dumpty was even more confusing than the Cheshire Cat when he said that words had no meaning except what *he* wished them to mean. I asked Louise whether something similar did not perhaps happen at times when she would listen to something I said and then appear to twist the meaning of my words. She answered rather resentfully 'Perhaps you're right, I hadn't thought of that'.

I said I felt that sometimes, while she was grumpy when I got it wrong, she was even grumpier when I got it right. It was very difficult for her to allow me to say something she had not thought about herself. I thought this might be one of the reasons why, in the past, she had got on so much better with books than with people. She got so much into the books she read that I wasn't sure she remembered that someone else had written them, whereas it was more difficult when I spoke with her to feel that my thoughts were *her* thoughts. She smiled in a way that I have come to recognise as an acknowledgement, but one mixed with a sort of 'It hurts!' This happened now very rarely. At the beginning of treatment, I often felt that Louise reacted to an interpretation as if she felt I wanted deliberately to hurt her or to assert some sort of superiority over her. Her perception of my words was filtered through the expectation of mockery and cruelty, which was very prominent in her internal reality.

By this time, she could experience psychic pain without feeling too persecuted by it. She seemed to realise that, if she wished to take Humpty Dumpty's assistance as a therapeutic aid, we needed to look together at aspects of herself that she might not like. She could see that it was necessary to understand whatever was spoiling or hindering the relationship with me in order to understand how often she might have spoiled or hindered other relationships in her life.

The Frog in the Milk

It was particularly important to help Louise to differentiate the (by now) sixteen-year-old part of her, which could work with me, from the more infantile part. I happened to know that she had not been a good feeder from early infancy (see also Chapter 7), and I have mentioned that she was also a very thin child. We could now observe the 'poor feeder' in her relationship with me, a little Louise who preferred at times not to like the food (i.e. food for thought) rather than say 'That is good'.

In a session at this time, I had been talking (certainly not for the first time) about this poor feeder, and Louise responded with a helpful association. She told me that at school they had been reading an amusing story, and I'm sure she knew that she was talking about herself in quoting the main character. He was a little boy called Nicholas, who was 'in disgrace' because he wouldn't eat his bread and milk. He said he would not eat it because there was a frog in it, and the whole family was up in arms because they all maintained there was no frog in Nicholas' bread and milk. But they were all proved wrong because there was indeed a frog in it – and not accidentally, either, because Nicholas had put it in himself. Louise laughed after telling me this story, and I think that at this point we had reached the stage where she could actually do some work herself and see that very often she put frogs in the 'bread and milk' that I offered her. Occasionally, she could see this without any help from me.

For instance, she now told me that often, at the beginning of treatment when she used to smile and I didn't know why, she was really having a little laugh within herself whenever I pronounced something with a peculiar accent; I'm sure this did happen quite often. On these occasions, she did not pay any attention to what I was saying because she was too busy making fun of me in her mind.

Louise did not smile secretively any longer, but I did not feel that we could stop worrying about the risk of her spoiling good experiences. I became fairly confident that something was unfolding within her – a function on the side of development, an antithesis of Humpty Dumpty. I have given two instances of hard work on her part. But my work with her had not come to an end. She still found it very difficult to make close acquaintance with the spoiling frog, and I shall conclude with an instance that points to her wish – a very understandable wish – to leave this task to me. It occurred in a session just prior to a holiday break. Although Louise was by then much less controlling, she certainly did not take kindly to a holiday. She obviously did not want me to leave her for a fortnight, especially in the company of an internal spoiling 'frog'. She told me, looking rather sullen, that I really seemed to be very keen on frogs, since I talked so much about them. She said I reminded her of the princess in the fairy tale who kisses the frog, hoping it will turn into a prince.

You may remember that, in that fairy tale, the frog (actually a toad) *does* turn into a prince. Here is an image that gives food for thought in terms of a definition of psychotherapy. Louise said she had been thinking about the fairy tale on her way to the session and decided it had a peculiar ending. She could not understand how the prince would want to have anything to do with the princess after his transformation. Then she smiled, and there was a touch of a very familiar grin on her face, mixed with an element of adolescent defiance. 'After all', she said, 'who would want to bother with somebody who goes about kissing frogs?'

2

Thinking and Learning in Deprived Children

Many children who have been in care for a substantial period of time especially early in their lives appear to suffer from learning difficulties. The problem is recurrent enough to suggest a link between early deprivation and the inadequacy in the internalisation of the equipment which is necessary for a child to acquire and retain knowledge; most of all, to think. In this chapter I try to outline some of the obstacles one encounters when attempting to facilitate such internalisation in deprived children. It is, incidentally, one of the reasons why their psychotherapy is a very long-term process.

Thinking is not to be seen as the unfolding of an autonomous function, but as deeply related to a child's emotional development. It often appears to be impaired in children who have suffered from the lack of a consistent caretaker holding their emotional needs and anxieties. Shuttleworth (1982, p. 76) describes a boy called Ian who defined himself by saying, 'I am bad, I am no good, I can't think'. She writes that Ian 'had been left with extremely inadequate mental resources to cope with a degree of pain which could overwhelm the most favourably brought up child'. If we reflect upon this statement we see that the problem is two-fold: good equipment would often be inadequate to negotiate the degree of pain deprived children are often confronted with. In many cases the equipment is, to start with, not adequate but faulty. I would like to focus, first, on the reasons why the equipment often appears to be faulty, and later on the issue of the intolerable input. I shall also draw a distinction between two-dimensional and hollow mental states.

Faulty Equipment

Wilfred Bion developed helpful insight into 'the world that is revealed by the attempt to understand our understanding' and the formulation of ideas by which thinking thoughts is achieved (Bion, 1962 paras VII & X). He suggests that a 'stepping stone' in the normal development of a child is the experience of 'a container', a person able to receive into herself (I am using the feminine as this function is often fulfilled by the mother or substitute mother) a chaotic input of feelings and sensations, mainly painful ones. These feelings need to be held and somehow made bearable for the infant through a process that initially takes place in 'the container'. For instance, the mother of a small baby might be confronted with a distressed infant who is crying and maybe even refusing to be fed although hungry. He is totally overwhelmed by a cluster of distress which is meaningless to him. If the mother is able to understand the reason for his discomfort, give it a meaning, and minister to the child's needs, she will perform for him what Bion describes as 'alpha function' (Bion, 1962, p. 2). By this he means that she will use her own empathy or 'reverie' (a process that involves feelings and thoughts as deeply interwoven with one another) in order to metabolise in herself what the child is not as yet able to metabolise. It is through this process, which takes place again and again during a child's infancy, that the chaotic cluster of painful feelings and sensations experienced by the baby as totally overwhelming can be responded to and made bearable. Bion describes this process as transforming unprocessed 'beta elements', often experienced purely at a 'protomental bodily level' into meaningful and thinkable 'alpha elements'. He stresses that it is vital, in this process, for the mother to use her own mental equipment for giving a meaning to the meaningless. Very gradually the child takes inside himself this repeated experience of having a space in somebody's mind and of being understood. It enables him to develop his own capacity to think and to develop a space *in his own mind.*

It should not be taken for granted that such a space exists from birth ready to receive the mental equivalent of food. Although I am making frequent comparisons with the digestive system in describing a child's mental development, I would like to stress that while a physically healthy child is born with a stomach and the equipment to digest food, there appears not to be an equivalent asset in mental development. The mental equipment and its capacity to metabolise contents develop only gradually. They are not born with the child. Unfavourable conditions may well interfere with their development. We are often confronted with patients, especially amongst those who have missed out on the early experience of 'containment' as described by Bion, who do not seem to have developed such equipment. This was the case with a girl who was thirteen when she started therapy and whom I treated inten-

2. *Thinking and Learning in Deprived Children*   27

sively for four years. Mandy had been in a children's home for the first six years of her life, but she had completely 'forgotten' those first six years.

At the beginning of treatment I felt that my words were somehow gliding away from her; I had the disconcerting feeling that she lacked a receptacle for her thoughts and feelings. She suffered from severe learning difficulties and was still a very poor reader when she started treatment. Very gradually, Mandy developed a rudimentary internal space and was able during some sessions to stay, at least fleetingly, with painful thoughts and feelings. She appeared to transform something that 'could be thought about' into bodily processes. This defence, which drained her of any insight she had acquired, could take the shape of vomiting or diarrhoea. At times I saw a version of the same phenomenon in her particular way of crying. I felt strongly that her eyes were crying in order to wash away the feelings but it was as if she didn't perceive it. She would often let her tears flow, occasionally blowing her nose while, as she told me herself, she didn't feel any pain. A memory which emerged only in her second year of treatment was that she had wet the bed until the age of ten; she also suffered at times from heavy vaginal haemorrhages. Mandy spoke anxiously about them, saying 'I feel the life blood is running out of me'. On investigation, an organic cause could be found for this last symptom only.

A haemorrhage, as opposed to vomiting and diarrhoea, provides a graphic image of the depleting process that often occurs in deprived children and is at the root of their thinking and learning difficulties. If a child consistently uses this evacuatory model in order to rid himself or herself of painful thoughts and emotions, 'the life blood', i.e. the capacity to think and learn, may be lost with the waste product. Deprived children rarely preserve a selective capacity to think, learn and retain notions so long as they use an excretory process for intolerable feelings or thoughts. If this were not so, learning difficulties would not be so frequent among them.

At the times when Mandy 'emptied and flattened herself' I had the feeling that she reverted from a short-lived three-dimensionality, from having an internal space, to two-dimensionality (Meltzer et al., 1975) as a defence against mental pain. This is, I think, a rather frequent occurrence especially when three-dimensionality or depth is only a recent and still precarious acquisition. At the beginning of treatment, and also when she reverted to two-dimensional shallowness, Mandy could relate to me only through 'adhesive identification', (Meltzer, 1975), that is, by precariously 'sticking' to me.

This modality was vividly portrayed when she told me, close to a holiday break, that she had got 'into a state' at school and 'couldn't understand why', when she had taken the clingwrap off her sandwiches and had seen it shrivel to nothing. The communication of the catastrophic feeling of 'shrivelling to nothing' and totally losing substance, when separated from a source of sustenance, was something I had lightly touched upon in my interpretations, without finding resonance in Mandy. In that particular session I could help her to emerge from her panic, as she was still 'in a state' when she arrived for her session, and had almost pleaded with me to help her make emotional sense of an utterly incomprehensible feeling. This was very rare at the time, as it involved the attempt to grasp the devastating symbolic meaning of an apparently trivial event.

I find it useful to differentiate paper-thin two-dimensional mental states from what I refer to as 'hollow' mental states. In my clinical experience, 'hollow' patients are more likely to have once possessed a containing space and then lost it or renounced it as a defence against psychic pain, rather than never having developed a reliable internal space, like Mandy. A vivid image of 'hollowness' was given by a little girl of eight, Sharon, who had spent a long time in care and who also suffered from learning difficulties. She made a plasticine baby, which had a hole passing through its body from its mouth to its 'wee-wee'. When this baby was 'fed' by her the water went straight through and out at the other end. Sharon was occasionally quite capable of thinking as Mandy was, but could not retain this capacity consistently. I think of 'hollowness' as intermediate between two-dimensional and three-dimensional, a state of mind when there is as yet only a fragile internal container whose 'floor' easily collapses. Bion (1962, p. 35) refers to the abdication of a potential 'alpha function' as follows: 'Intolerance of frustration could be so pronounced that alpha function would be forestalled by an immediate evacuation of beta elements'. In my view, this process can lead either to a state of hollowness or to a secondary, often only temporary collapse into two-dimensionality. I have often encountered this defensive strategy in patients haunted by internal persecutors: the collapse of the internal space (cf. the two sides of a balloon adhering to one another when the air comes out) serves the function of temporarily evicting intolerable 'tenants'.

Intolerable Input

Having discussed the issue of faulty equipment for thinking, I would now like to return to the problem of the degree of pain. The overwhelming mental pain and catastrophic fears aroused by repeated changes of caretakers were vividly conveyed by Simon, who was eight when he started treatment with a colleague and who had been through a nightmarish sequence of 'in and out' of care and changes of care. Near the beginning of his treatment Simon asked his therapist, almost as if anticipating an abrupt ending, whether he would be coming forever. 'How long is forever? Why don't we fall off the earth? If we fell off the earth and fell and fell would we fall forever?', he asked. He said he thought that his therapist would move and get another job like Mr X, who had just left the children's home, and he added sadly: 'As soon as you get used to things they change'. Simon expressed with great vividness the cruelty that he felt was inflicted on him by losses, and holiday breaks in therapy were always dramatic. In a session close to a Christmas break he scribbled on a piece of paper 'a plant grows in the soil' and then 'RSPCA', which he quickly changed to 'RSPCB' (meaning 'cruelty to babies').

At the time when yet another change of children's home loomed as a threat on the horizon, he sang in a session: 'We are making plans for Simon – Simon must be happy, be happy when he dies'. The message appeared to be: 'You are at risk of death if you put down roots in the soil of a relationship. You know that you will suddenly be uprooted and there is no RSPCB to protect you'. The bitterness of Simon's song is chilling and gives an opening to understand another communication of this child. His awareness that his therapist was becoming a central person in his life made him feel almost attacked by her, as this made him vulnerable to future unavoidable pain. On one occasion, as the therapist was attempting to make contact with him, he drowned her voice by singing the song, 'It's cruel to be kind'. We have seen that Simon had preserved and was at times capable of using a capacity to think, but he also slipped into mindlessness when the pain became unbearable. Soiling was one of his symptoms and it increased considerably when he needed to evacuate his thoughts and feelings. Needless to say, learning difficulties also featured amongst his symptoms.

We will see, in Chapter 3, how my patient Martin becomes extremely skilled at breaking links and executing thoughts, in his mind and between our minds, as a defence against psychic pain. Martin's approach to ridding himself of thoughts was much more violent than

Mandy's sliding into mindlessness and two-dimensionality, but whether thoughts are 'executed' or evacuated, the damage to mental functioning is massive. A significant consequence that is present in both instances is that feelings of pining, of missing the valued object in its absence, are by-passed in so far as the memory of its existence is obliterated. We saw how Mandy had been capable of obliterating six years of her life through 'forgetting'; Martin similarly asked me to help him forget that I existed, especially close to a break. References to a forthcoming break, but even more my very presence in the room, were treated as unwelcome reminders of my not being dead, buried, obliterated, or 'executed'. Martin was at times quite aware of the murderous rage evoked by my disappearances, both between sessions and during breaks. You will see that he tells me on one occasion, 'If I am not in control, all you have got is the choice of death, hanging, electric chair, drowning or decapitation'. (Decapitation being perhaps the most significant of my options in the context of what I am addressing here.)

This 'out of sight out of mind', or perhaps 'murdered in mind', procedure can be a significant contributory factor to the impaired development of a capacity for thought. Bion (1962) suggests that the latter develops initially through an attempt to keep an object alive in the mind when absent. He actually stresses the importance of experiencing the absence as a spur to formulating the thoughts, that is, to thinking about a mother who is *not* there. This process can successfully take place if the frustration to be tolerated is congruous with the child's equipment at various levels of development. Children exposed to frequent and repeated losses may find it intolerable to keep alive the many 'absent objects' in their lives. They are attacked or obliterated.

The space once occupied by the good present object does not remain vacant (Bion, 1962). The tenants of the empty space are now attacking and persecutory because they have been fiercely attacked in phantasy. They are often perceived as internal monsters, and this can help us understand the overwhelming anxieties of many deprived children. Their internal world is a graveyard milling with frightening ghosts. When alone, they are not really alone, but in the company of their internal persecutors. It appears to me, moreover, that one of the reasons for reverting from three-dimensionality to two-dimensionality which I spoke of earlier in this chapter is the defensive obliteration of an internal space, perceived not only as a receptacle for painful thoughts and feelings, but also for nightmarish tenants that need to be evicted.

This understandable defence can help us formulate a hypothesis about the impoverishment of phantasy as well as thought in deprived children. These children may be using a self-defeating mechanism that faces them with a 'double deprivation' (Henry [Williams], 1974 and Chapter 3). In addition to their external, often massive deprivation, they are faced with a lack of imagination, vitality, capacity to think and to learn. An internal space is a luxury which they might, for a long time, be unable to afford. A very arduous task is undertaken in treatment in the attempt to restore the texture of a patient's internal world, and facilitate the internalisation of a benevolent object which can provide support from within when facing panic and anxiety and increase the capacity to tolerate psychic pain.

3
Double Deprivation

The theme of this chapter will be what I have termed 'double deprivation', and which I will illustrate with material from my work with Martin, a patient whom I saw on a non-intensive basis. There was first a deprivation inflicted upon him by external circumstances over which he had no control whatsoever. Second, there was a deprivation deriving from internal sources: from his crippling defences and from the quality of his internal objects, which provided him with so little support that he was made an orphan inwardly as well as outwardly. Martin was referred at the age of fourteen for aggressive behaviour, stealing and considerable learning difficulties. His reading age was six. He had made a suicide attempt two years prior to referral, when he tried to jump from a second floor window.

History

Martin was the illegitimate child of Afro-Caribbean parents, and had been placed in care at the age of two months. His mother died when he was seven years old, but she had had no contact with Martin after he went into care. His father had disappeared at the beginning of the mother's pregnancy. Martin had three placements up to the age of two, when he was fostered by an English couple with a child of their own, a boy four years older than Martin. He was with the foster parents for ten years until fostering broke down at the age of twelve. It seems that the foster parents found Martin increasingly unmanageable because of his stealing and very defiant behaviour, and they had reached the point where they felt 'unable to accept him or have any trust in him'. There is no indication of the impact that the attempted suicide one year before the breakdown of fostering might have had on the foster parents, and how it might possibly have contributed to their feeling at a loss. However, they reported that the difficulties with Martin had considerably increased from the time when he was informed of his natural mother's death.

When Martin left the foster home he returned to a children's home and there were apparently no outward signs of his being distressed about the move. There are, however, many indications in the case history of the foster parents' deep feeling of failure in their relationship with Martin. They saw his coldness and detachment as confirmation that they had never meant a great deal to him. The first contact after the move to the children's home was a phone call which had to be cut short because the foster mother was crying so much that she could not talk. Both foster parents visited Martin at the home but their son refused to join them because 'Martin had hurt his mother too much'. After meeting Martin they left feeling that 'nothing had happened. He appeared to have happily settled himself down'. They said they would prefer to discontinue contact with Martin and completely lost touch with him since. I have described the breaking down of fostering in some detail as it is relevant to my main issue of this paper: the 'double deprivation' I mentioned at the beginning of the chapter.

Identification with an Idealised Internal Object

When Martin started treatment he had spent just over a year at the children's home and was attending a large secondary school. The most alarmed and alarming reports came initially from the school, where Martin had become dangerously aggressive to other children. In spite of careful daily inspections, he had developed a talent for smuggling knives into the school and suddenly flicking them open, terrorising other children. On one occasion, which had been followed by suspension, he had pointed a knife at a child's throat and the child had very nearly fainted with fear. Martin did not seem to show any reaction to punishments or reproaches. While provoking violent emotions in others, he himself appeared to be, most of the time, devoid of feelings. As he was to tell me some months later, 'a teacher at my old school said that I am the only person he has come across who has *no* feelings'.

When I first met Martin, I also perceived an alarming quality of numbness about him. It was as if, although the suicide attempt he made two years earlier had not succeeded, he was really only going through the motions of being alive, the motions of coming for treatment, very regularly and punctually (in fact he was invariably early), without being in the least in touch with his motivations for coming. His environment was indeed highly motivated on his behalf and, at that time, carrying the weight of all the feelings Martin was not perceiving himself. In fact his numbness was, at least in part, a consequence of his enormous skill in splitting off and disposing of feelings or parts of himself into other people, unfortunately in a very scattered way, as in the terrorising of children at school.

There was only one thing in life which Martin seemed to invest with enormous importance and this was his appearance. I had heard before he started treatment that he often took more than one hour getting ready before going out, and the care he put into the most minute details showed at first sight, even when he was in a school uniform. When I saw him during a school holiday, I had a better opportunity to catch glimpses of his personal taste. He paid an enormous amount of attention to the choice of colours; the matching or contrasting of pink and pale green, of various shades of red and orange; he often wore bracelets; chains with a pendant; for a brief period he started wearing one ear-ring. He had many rings on each hand; some of them looked fairly harmless, but at times he arrived at his sessions with a full set of knuckle rings. It made a particularly striking contrast when he was wearing pale and rather feminine colours. Martin had a very handsome face, but at first it was very mask-like and showed little change of expression. His hair was short, carefully divided in the middle with a straight parting, and slightly puffed on the sides. As I have often seen him use a comb during sessions, I know that this puffing involved an elaborate procedure; a sort of back-combing made very difficult by his frizzy hair.

I mentioned earlier the disconcerting, unreachable quality I perceived in Martin at the beginning of treatment. There was *always* a feeling of his not being all there, which made it very difficult to establish contact with him. But I gradually came to realise that there was often a specific mood attached to the lack of contact. While not listening, or treating whatever I said as if he perceived only a remote sound, he appeared to be totally absorbed in a detail of his appearance; at times it might be something very minor, like removing tiny specks of dust or fluff from his jacket; at times his movements became feminine, almost in a caricatured way. For instance, using his sun glasses as a mirror, he could spend lengthy periods smoothing his eyebrows with his fingertips; or he could become totally absorbed in the care of his nails. Once he came to his session with nail varnish on the nails of both hands. On those occasions he treated my attempts to reach him with an interpretation as if I were a sort of annoying child, or a noise in the background: I should not disturb him while he was busy with something, which was so much more important than anything I could possibly say. Indeed, the identification with an idealised internal object was, at this time, very important to him, being, precarious as it was, the only thing which held him together.

One particular session provides a vivid example of the type of projective identification I was confronted with, a form of entering inside an object like a hand into a glove puppet similar to the examples given by Melanie Klein in 'On Identification' (Klein, 1955).

Martin was wearing an anorak with a fur-trimmed hood; I was to learn later that its name (it could not be more appropriate in the context) is a 'parka'. He pulled the hood right over his head, then took a comb out of his pocket and started combing the long-haired fur around his hood as if he were curling it with long, sensuous, feminine strokes. He really behaved as if he perceived himself 'parked' inside someone else's skin. The impact of his behaviour was heightened by the fact that on this occasion, as on many others, he was wearing menacing rings on his right hand fingers, but seemed completely oblivious of them.

In this session, and in the ones I have previously described, his verbal responses to my attempts to reach him were in the nature of 'Yes, what is it you wanted to say?', 'I have got no time for your rubbish', 'Tough, you have got to suffer', 'You are talking to a brick wall'. His tone of voice was cold, contemptuous and very hard. Indeed it *was* like talking to a brick wall, and after some trials and errors, I realised that this was the most important quality of Martin's communication: that he had to put me in the position of the child who tries to make contact with somebody who has no time to listen, a hard and vain mother who says, 'Tough, you have got to suffer', while she is curling her hair and treats with scorn and contempt the weakling who is trying to get some of her attention. I am referring to Martin's internal object, but it also appeared, from subsequent material, to be the phantasy that he had formed about the reason why his mother had left him just after his birth: that she was too vain, hard and self-centred to care for a small baby.

The purpose of Martin's unreachable attitude was now, as it had probably been many times in the past, the one of splitting and projecting into somebody else both the feelings that he could not tolerate and a part of himself, the needy child he had to disown; at the same time he identified himself with the unavailable object *which at this time he idealised*, felt completely at one with, and thus in control of.

When I said to Martin that I thought he behaved with me as if I were a nuisance child, trying to talk to a mother who is only interested in the reflection of her face in the mirror and can't be bothered to listen, a very hard mother, like a brick wall, he answered: 'There is only one way to find out whether you are a brick wall or not. You hit your head against a brick wall; if it hurts, you are not'. The implication of this statement is very enlightening in terms of the development of Martin's defences. He appeared to be saying that the only way *not* to get hurt, if you have got this type of object, is to identify with it, become a brick wall yourself and leave the hurt to someone else. The use of this type of defence brought about the numbness I referred to above, both through identification with an insensitive internal object, and through a depletion due to the splitting of feelings and parts of himself into other people. After all, the foster mother, *not Martin*, was crying on the phone, while he behaved 'as if nothing had happened', and it was the foster parents who subsequently made themselves unavailable for further contact. This chain reaction of rejection had probably occurred many times in Martin's life.

The pressure Martin could put on an external object to give up trying, to give up any hope that he could be reached, was very strong. I think that the forceful impact he had on people in this respect must have deprived him, many times, of positive experiences. He had developed a talent not only for hardening himself, but *for hardening people around him* and making them deaf to the real nature of his need. Any further deprivation and experience of an external hard object was reintrojected and cemented the hardness of his internal object.

The Pakistani

It is understandable that Martin should have such dread of getting in touch with feelings of dependency, when he had inside himself a very insensitive object and he had so often contributed to hardening his external objects. He was not as yet sure that this would not also happen with me, although the sentence I quoted earlier on implied at least a hope that I might bear the impact of his behaviour, and *not* become a brick wall.

Martin's profound contempt and hatred for a split-off, needy part of himself has been a recurrent theme in treatment; it was initially to be known to us as 'the Pakistani'. Martin's prejudice against Pakistanis was fierce and sanctimonious and he had often chosen Pakistani children as the target of his attacks in school. He used to say about them: 'They can't fend for themselves, or they wouldn't have come over here for help, would they?' 'They are inferior, they are savages, not like us British'. This inferior and needy savage had not only to be despised, but crushed and obliterated: 'Oh, I love Pakistanis', Martin said once, 'you hit them and they come for more and more and more until you kill them', and he menacingly caressed the knuckle rings which covered all the fingers on his right hand. It was probably very similar to what he felt would happen to the weakling, the fool who kept hitting his head against an insensitive hard mother; he would not survive it for long. Subsequent material brought much more into the open Martin's anxieties about death, but he was using as 'receptacles' (cf. Chapter 8) the children he terrorised in school with knives. This type of acting out fluctuated, but it ceased completely at the beginning of the second year of treatment, when signs of integration of this split-off part began to emerge. Martin told me one day: 'I'm not after all the Pakistanis in the world, I'm not man-hunting, I am just after one bloke'. Then he started scribbling. On the side of his box he wrote *his* name, *his* address, and *his* telephone number.

Grievances

As, gradually and very tentatively, Martin began to realise that the Pakistani he had been bashing, despising and depriving of the help he needed was within himself and he caught the first glimpses of insight into this area of need, of wanting help, and wishing me to retrieve him when he lost touch (the address and the telephone number), so he began to reproach me increasingly for hardness, coldness, and negligence, in failing to provide what he needed. he could idealise the aloof, detached, narcissistic quality of his object, only as long as he kept the needy child completely split off. While he used this defence, he *was* the insensitive mother, completely identifying with her. The feelings that she evoked had to be felt by the despised, trampled Pakistanis, not by him.

As he began to perceive *his* feelings of need, he also got in touch with *his* grievances. His appearance mirrored very strikingly his changed state of mind and the shift in his identifications. He would at times come to the Clinic wearing trousers too short for him, a torn jumper, holes in his socks. In the session previous to a holiday break, he was wearing a very thick 'second skin' (Bick, 1968): a shirt, two jumpers, a cardigan and his anorak although it was not a very cold day. As soon as he sat down, he touched the radiator as if shivering and said: 'Call this central heating? Cold water running through a mass of metal'. When I linked this reproach for coldness, and his holding himself together with many protective layers, to the forthcoming holiday break, Martin moved to an eroticised and much safer area of grievances: he said I was such a cold person, because I came from a cold country (he was convinced I was Polish) and all we have in Poland is snow and ice, while he comes from Africa where they have beautiful tropical fishes and sunshine. While saying that, his attitude became very seductive, as if he wished to imply that he had all the warmth, the passion, the glamour of Africa, as opposed to me – a metallic object with cold water in my veins (the mass of metal with cold water running through it).

On occasion, the grievances had a marked defensive quality to them, and Martin appeared to go to great lengths to put himself in a position where he could reproach me for neglect. From the very first days of treatment, he had come very early to the Clinic, at least half and hour, often an hour earlier than his 10 o'clock appointment. We knew from the houseparents that he always left home after breakfast at eight o'clock and that he often walked all the way to the Clinic (about four miles) in order to save his fare money. The reasons for coming early were different at different times in treatment; the behaviour remained the same, but its meaning changed many times over the first two years. At the time when grievances began to emerge, coming early appeared to serve a specific purpose. No matter how punctual I was, from Martin's point of view, I had kept him waiting a long time; I was not available when he arrived. It is true that I *had* kept him waiting since the previous session and the sessions were weekly, and thus very far apart. Martin would look very sullen as he left the waiting room. He often brought a comic along and would look through it for the first two or three minutes or look outside the window, very much out of touch with me, then suddenly turn towards the clock, which had obviously moved from ten o'clock and remark for instance: 'Late again', or shrug his shoulders as if to say: 'You are hopeless'. On one occasion he said, referring to the previous session, 'You were half a minute late last time'.

I think that the main defensive purpose served by the grievances was that Martin felt much more comfortable in a known situation, confronted with somebody whom he did not value, someone who could be no good and no use to him, somebody not to be trusted. This was a dimension in which he moved with great ease, a very familiar one. He had not really trusted anybody in his life, and was not prepared to take chances. For instance, his defensive projective identification with the internal insensitive mother had an enormous advantage over a relationship with any live object. It could be conjured up at any moment; it was always available and Martin felt in full control, while he could not fall back on my help all the time. At first, in fact, he could only do that for fifty minutes out of all the hours in the week, and I wondered about a reference to the seven days of the week when he told me once that he had 'seven layers of skin that covered the soft spot': not just a 'crust of the weekend' but a crust of the week. I decided that, as soon as I had a vacancy, I would offer him a second session. Martin reacted to the offer by saying that he would only come if he could choose the day and time. Why couldn't I see him on Saturday mornings? Why couldn't the Clinic stay open at weekends? Anyhow he did not need to come twice a week, in fact he did not even need to come once. His spasmodic need to be in control was very clearly spelled out: 'If I were not in control I would not be here', 'If I am not in control, all you have got is the choice of death: hanging, electric chair, drowning, decapitation'.

I thought at first that it would be better to allow him to work through his anxieties and wait for the time when he would be able to say that he wished to accept the second session, but I came to realise that, were he able to say so openly that he needed more help, he would not be so ill and in need of it. In fact, to my surprise, he seemed very relieved when eventually I arranged for him to have a second session without waiting for his blessing. Indeed, he always appeared to experience relief when there was an acknowledgement, in the outside world, of how little he could as yet look after himself and his needs.

Although I felt that it was worthwhile to disrupt the rhythm of treatment in order to increase the sessions, I realised that this change in the known pattern had temporarily shaken Martin's feeling of safety in the therapeutic 'setting' (Meltzer, 1967). I also think that the increased number of sessions was at first experienced as a rather cruel tantalising game. If I could give him a little more, then why so little? For instance, Martin brought to one of his sessions the advertisement for a restaurant 'open most hours of the day and night', providing me with a model of how things should be. One day, looking at the 'emergency numbers' on the telephone dial and talking about emergencies, he said: 'But I am not an emergency, am I? Or I would come every day'. He referred to the time of the session as 'miserable fifty minutes', and told me, after I had referred to myself as 'mother' in a transference interpretation, that 'there are no mothers in a place like this' – he referred to the Clinic and, I expect, just as much to a children's home – 'only people doing their job and getting paid for it. There might be some mothers, but that means they have got children at home'.

This reproach about me being no more than yet another part-time person in his life was a very recurrent one. It always appeared to imply that if I put him in touch with a feeling of need, if I was responsible for his knowing that he had a soft spot *inside* himself and not lodged in any odd Pakistani, I could help him only by offering the actual mothering he had been deprived of, or deprived himself of, and a very idealised, always available mothering at that. I should not expose him to the pain of knowing what he had missed without providing it, in the present, if not in the past. Whenever I fell short of those expectations, and I was bound to *all the time*, I was felt to be playing a cruel tantalising game. I came to understand only later that Martin's repeated accusations that I wanted to make him cry were, at least partly, serving the purpose of turning me into the executioner and himself into the victim who was only fighting in self-defence and was, thus, immune to guilt.

Physical and Mental Violence

Towards the end of the first year of treatment, while reproaching me for cruelty, Martin threatened me on a number of occasions with physical violence. A key session in this respect was one very close to our first Christmas break. He had spoken and complained about the rain on his way to the Clinic, and he had referred to the doll's house (an open plan one in the corner), saying: 'That house is no good: it would let the rain in'. He had put his face out of the window (it was still raining), and wiped his face afterwards. I said that he seemed to be talking about getting his face wet with tears, that he felt that, like the doll's house, I did not provide enough protection against the 'rain-tears'. Martin caressed his knuckle rings with a smile as if getting ready to punch me and said: 'You can get your face wet with rain, with tears, with blood, and yours is going to be wet with blood before mine is wet with tears'. It might be relevant that the risk of physical violence being acted out or, better, 'acted in' treatment (Meltzer, 1967) coincided with the end of aggressive behaviour elsewhere. The problem came to be gathered more in the transference. Although physical violence did not ever actually occur, I think that Martin needed to bring about a situation where I would take very seriously the possibility that it could occur and bear the feelings that this aroused.

I found both of Mary Boston's papers (1967, 1972) on her work with a patient from a children's home most helpful in highlighting problems which may be recurrent in the treatment of institutionalised children. Mary Boston (1972, p. 6) refers to the patient's phantasy, greatly reinforced by reality, that his hostile impulses might be responsible for the parents' disappearance and points out: 'Understanding the hostility and phantasies may not be sufficient. The new object, the therapist, has to prove that he can contain the violence and reduce its omnipotence by withstanding it and surviving as the original object in the patient's phantasy did not' (1972). This issue is very relevant in Martin's case. I came to know that his anxieties about the extent of his omnipotence were very strong and that it is certainly possible that his disturbance became exacerbated when he heard of his mother's death because it was experienced by him as a further confirmation, in reality, of the power of his murderous phantasies. He had told me that I would only have the choice of death if I escaped his control. His mother did and she died. Other very overwhelming feelings had also been aroused by her death, as it shattered all hopes that she would ever come back and it was experienced by Martin as the ultimate proof of her narcissistic, selfish withdrawal. Very close to one of my holiday breaks, he said bitterly, 'She is having a lovely holiday, pushing up the daisies' (on her grave).

At the time when Martin was threatening me with his knuckle rings or, suddenly, when he flicked a knife open and stabbed his box[1] ('We'll have to get a new box', 'We'll have to get a new Mrs Williams'), he spoke about his mother having died of 'foot and mouth disease' and produced many other gruesome sadistic phantasies. Very divorced from his feelings, they had a ruminatory quality to them and I often felt it appropriate to interrupt the ruminations. He called them his 'walks in the graveyard' and they provided an image of the large portion of his internal world which resembled a graveyard. In those instances there was not a glimpse of guilt feelings, as *I* was supposed to feel all the guilt for wanting to make him cry, as his mother had wanted to make him cry. I was confronted with the grievances of a lifetime; he behaved as if he were either phantasising attacks or threatening physical violence in self-defence.

Once the threat of physical violence receded, the impact of the violence did not diminish. It remained as mental violence, but to a certain extent it became easier to work. It is very difficult indeed to gather one's thoughts and interpret when a knife can suddenly appear out of nowhere. (The strength of his projections was enhanced by the surprise element.) Martin let me know that this type of danger was over in a way which was typical of how he showed me he had gained a piece of insight: he gave it back to me in a patronizing sort of way. While talking I was quite unaware of moving my hands. Martin touched one of my hands with a finger, gently pressing it towards the table and said:

---

[1] At the beginning of treatment he was provided with a cardboard box which he seldom opened. It contained drawing material, a ball of string, etc.

'We can just talk, you don't need to use your hands'. By projection *I* had become the acting out patient.

On this occasion I also think that eroticisation of the relationship (touching my hand, the seductive behaviour, the quality of innuendo in Martin's words) had been used as a defence; in this case against tender feelings. Indeed, Martin found any feelings of warmth, closeness, tenderness so painful that he had to dispose of them very quickly. Either he eroticised them and turned them into excitement or he had to 'execute' them. 'My hurt is not my business. I execute it', he once said while fiercely cutting a piece of string that he was holding in his hands in two halves with his own pen knife. I think that this sign language provides a very good example of the 'attacks on linking' described by Bion (1959) which were a core of the mental violence in Martin and, possibly, one of the greatest sources of his deprivation.

In 'Attacks on Linking', Bion (1959, p. 102) says: 'I employ the term link because I wish to discuss the patient's relationship with a function, rather than with the object that subserves a function; my concern is not only with the breast or penis or verbal thought, but with their function of providing a link between two objects'. Elsewhere, in the same paper, Bion compares this shift of focus as paying attention to physiology as different from anatomy.

If, using the model proposed by Bion, I attempt to summarise the three most frequent 'attacks on linking' that occurred in Martin's treatment, I shall refer firstly to his emptying of meaning, and thus of feeling, a piece of insight he had just acquired: *attacks on links within his mind.*

He used this method as the quickest remedy against any painful feelings as he much preferred to be in a muddle than to be in pain. He could achieve this purpose by taking a word out of context and 'executing it'. To quote an example: after he had emerged from one of his delusional identifications with the 'vain mother' and, for a moment, seemed really to feel and to understand how little sustenance this narcissistic object could provide for him, there was an abrupt change of mood. He took out of context the word 'character' that I had just used in connection with the vain mother and said, 'Character, character? Oh yes, I like carrots'. It was as quick and sudden as the flicking open of knives. In no time the meaning and the feeling were executed; the part of Martin that knew where it hurts and why it hurts was executed; and the consequence was *a loss of contact between his mind and my mind.*

This loss of contact is the second type of attack on linking to which I wish to refer. Martin was very much in need of a container (Bion,

1962), for the feelings he could not bear himself and of the experience that they could be survived, understood and processed for him by an external object. Bion suggests that a very extensive use in treatment of this type of projective identification, 'a stepping stone in development', probably implies that patients have been cheated of the use of this mechanism in infancy. In my view, it is very likely that this might frequently apply to children cared for in institutions. But being given what has been needed for so long is often accompanied by very painful feelings. As Bion points out: 'The patient feels he is being allowed an opportunity of which he had hitherto been cheated: the poignancy of the deprivation is thereby rendered the more acute and so are the feelings of resentment at the deprivation' (1959, pp. 104–5). I think that the rapid 'execution' of feelings of being understood, of being in touch, and the consequent loss of contact with me were defences against this type of painful experience.

A third type of attack, intimately connected with the first two, was aimed at *disrupting links within my mind*. Martin very openly expressed his intolerance of my being anything more than a passive container for his projections. 'You are just a great big dustbin stuffed with rubbish: dustbins don't talk'. 'If you find out something about me, just keep it to yourself, will you?' He was fighting against my not fitting in with a purely receptive role and my attempt to understand the meaning of what was happening. There the disruption often started. On some occasions my sentences were interrupted after the first two or three words, especially if I started a sentence with the words: 'I think that …'. 'You think everything, don't you?', he would say, or 'You are a brain-box'. He did not, as yet, know the content of my sentence; he was fighting the thinking, not the thoughts. If I stopped talking, as a silence was undoubtedly preferable to a battle of wits, he would say, 'Come on – proceed – what is it you were trying to say? Can't you remember?' Indeed this behaviour was not only an attack but a meaningful communication. Martin was once more telling me about a very destructive part of himself, another version of the 'Paki-basher' that was paralysing *his* capacity to think and showing me how it happened. The whole painful issue of the impaired use of his mind, of his incapacity to retain knowledge ('Can't you remember?'), to link and to learn was being put across.

I often interpreted this behaviour as a communication, but there was in fact something very crucial in those disruptions which was intended as an attack. Its nature appeared to me very similar to the quality of attacks described by Bion (1962) as follows:

The couple engaged in a creative act are felt to have an enviable emotional experience. He (the patient) being identified with the excluded
party, has a painful emotional experience. On many occasions the patient
... had a hatred of emotions and, therefore, by a short extension of life
itself. This hatred contributed to the murderous attacks on that which
links the pair, on the pair itself and on the object generated by the pair.
(Bion, 1962, p. 100)

And elsewhere:

... envy and hatred of a capacity for understanding, was leading him to
take in a good understanding object, in order to destroy and eject it, a
procedure which had often led to persecution by the destroyed and
ejected object. (Bion, 1962, p. 97)

In my opinion, Martin expressed something which can be understood
along those lines when he said, 'I want to overwork that little man that
runs around your head, putting together all the data. Why don't you
give him a holiday?' 'Why didn't I throw him out of the window and
let him have a bit of fresh air?' The attack on linking is here spelled out
as a wish to get rid of my 'little man', to disrupt the combined object,
to break the link (which in this case appears to be represented by the
paternal presence inside the mother) and thus make a creative process
impossible. A very primitive type of jealousy and envy, as well as
intolerance of psychic pain, were bringing about Martin's repeated
attempts at deadening the life of his object and he was left with a very
lifeless, cold and frightening object inside. The work of resuscitation
took a long time.

It was important for Martin to reach some understanding of the
connections between his attacks in the transference and the deadly
nature of his internal object. His impairment in learning, in spite of the
evidence he gave in his destructiveness of having a good mind, was
certainly connected with the fragmentation of his internal world. He
had been confronted daily, throughout his life, with this deprivation; in
this case, fortunately, a reversible one. It is, however, certainly relevant
that Martin had himself experienced so many broken links during the
first two years of his life. In the turnover of staff within the same
institution, and in the three changes of placements, he must so often
have lost people he had made some contact with.

First Glimpses of the Wish to be Retrieved

During this second year of treatment, especially in the second half, there were many indications that Martin was relying on my work to re-establish links when they were broken, so that he would not be allowed to get lost in his muddle or otherwise drift away. Although he let me know that he had gained some insight in this area in his manic, patronising way, he had still caught a glimpse of it. 'I have read the Bible', he told me, 'and it says there: "He who muddles shall perish in the eternal flames and he who speaks the truth shall live forever".' He also told me that 'you can put a piece of rope to all sorts of good uses, for instance you need it to tie a boat to the shore, so that it doesn't drift away, or you can tie the rope to a buoy'. As soon as he became aware of the double meaning of the word he laughed and said, 'I know what you are going to say'. In the same session, using the string for pulling the curtains, he showed me a very safe knot used by mountain climbers which he tied round both his legs; he said it was safe because it had a double loop. (Some acknowledgement, perhaps, that it is safer to be held by both parents?)

He said that even if he threw himself out of the window he would not fall, he would just hang by his legs. The reference to his attempted suicide was striking, but, as Martin never mentioned it directly, I did not refer to it in my interpretations. There was plenty of material in the sessions that put us in touch with his suicidal impulses and, at this stage, with his fear of them. Martin often asked me why did I not just 'let him rot in peace'; he said: 'Six feet underground is a peaceful place', 'The brain only stops working when you are dead', 'Dead people lose life, but they gain death'. He also said: 'If I were to kill myself, I know the quickest way of doing it. You jump out of a window, head first'. Very often these 'attacks on linking' during a session, his throwing his mind and feelings out of the window and the deadening of his object had a suicidal quality of brutal anaesthesia. I could talk about his suicidal impulses during the session.

However, I do not think that Martin would have dared me to let him drift away into madness or actual death without having developed some trust in an object that would not let it happen. During the second year of treatment, there were indications that he could at times experience a greater feeling of trust towards me and that he was capable, although in a rather intermittent way, of a more dependent relationship. It is possible that this development might have been accelerated by events external to treatment which made him feel at risk.

Martin was supposed to leave the children's home when he was sixteen and over the years he had often said that he wished to join the Army. A great deal of material about the meaning the Army had for him had been brought to his sessions; it stood at first for a 'licence to kill', then more clearly for a 'licence to get killed' – 'a passport to death', as he called it. Although he himself felt much less motivated to join the Army, which would obviously have meant the end of treatment, initially nobody in his environment questioned his 'vocation'. Martin no longer gave cause for concern either at school or at the home, and from the external point of view he had made good progress; if he could pass the exams and join the Regulars, all were in agreement that he should. Martin brought the problem quite openly to sessions when he asked me, 'So what's going to happen when I am sixteen?', and also by bringing to the Clinic a picture of one of the homes where he had stayed as a small child. On another occasion he brought a leaflet on 'Local Authority Council and Related Services' and browsed through it, pointing at the 'Territorial and Army Volunteer Reserve' and saying, 'We don't want that, do we?' Then he looked at length at the page listing Child Care and Child Guidance.

I knew that Martin would not have been able to say openly, to anybody as yet, that he still needed a great deal of 'child care and child guidance'. In fact, I was surprised that he had gone as far as implying it. I felt a strong pressure towards taking direct steps to relieve his worry about the future, but it seemed more useful for me to deal in treatment with the strong anxieties this situation aroused in him. It was very fortunate that I could rely on a great deal of support from colleagues at the Clinic in putting across to the houseparents, the school and representatives of Social Services, how undesirable it would be for Martin to stop treatment at this stage and join the Army. However, one of the problems was where should he go instead; luckily a suitable post or placement could be found. It was also suggested by the school that he could stay on for six months after school-leaving age because he had developed a great interest in photography and he would be able to have some professional training in it.

It was important, in my view, for Martin to know that other people at the Clinic were concerned with the practical arrangements in his life. If he had felt that I was organising his future, I think he might have experienced this change in the known pattern as very confusing and tantalising. His reaction to the offer of the second session had given me food for thought in this respect. The crucial problem, if a change of technique is introduced at a given stage during treatment, is the need to set the limit again at some point, and to choose at which point to do so. It would have been very difficult to set a limit which made sense to Martin as to how far I could go and what I could actually do for him, if I had overstepped my role to the least degree. If I was taking care of his future placements, he might well have wondered why I did not offer him a home myself. Because of the extent of his deprivation and his craving for the 'full-time mother' that he could never have in external reality, I believed I could better help him by setting clear limits on what he could expect. If any change were possible, he could start again hoping that I might, at some stage, make up for *all* he had missed; in fact I could only help him lessen the extent of the deprivation which derived from internal sources.

There is an indication that Martin must have had some positive experiences in his early days because otherwise he would have been more impervious to treatment. When he first came it was difficult to get in touch with his wish to stay alive, but it *is* significant that he had not become psychotic (although he used a profusion of psychotic defences), that he *had* stayed alive. Spitz's (1945) work tells us about babies in similar circumstances who did not; Martin had cried for help by producing alarming symptoms, while other institutionalised children go through life dead or hollow inside, without anybody noticing it. At the point when Martin, having gathered his disturbance into treatment, offered a well-adjusted image to the environment and was considered to be fit for the Army, I realised what risks institutionalised children run when they offer the appearance of being intact.

It was a hopeful sign that in the instance I have just mentioned, Martin appeared to be able to stand on the side of his real need and to ask for more 'child care and child guidance'. It seemed to me an indication that he was by now in touch with an object within himself who could treat his needs with respect, and ask for them to be taken seriously; a role which he had completely left to me in the past. In fact Martin impoverished, depleted and deprived himself; through the use of splitting and projection, both of the good and bad parts of his self and object. The progressive reintegration which took place afforded hope that Martin's deprivation could gradually be lessened.

It cannot be denied, though, that Martin had also been *deprived* of something by our work. The previous changes of placement had probably been relatively painless. He let himself be moved like a suitcase, a fairly empty one, and left the tears to someone else (remember the foster mother?). But the move from the children's home was hard. When the prospective foster parents came to take him to their house for a weekend, they found him very cosily tucked up in bed with the blanket up to his nose, engrossed in reading a book. He said that he would prefer for the break to be definite, he wanted to go to their house and stay there, not come and go. He was then asked whether he would agree to go to them if he could bring something that mattered with him; as he was so engrossed in reading, would he like to bring that book? Martin answered that he would only go if he could take all his 'family' (house parents) with him. Fortunately it was possible to arrange for him to have regular contact with his house parents (he said he wished to see them once a week), but it is undeniable that the move was yet another loss in his life, and by now he had shed some of the protective layers that made him quite immune to any feelings of loss.

Early in treatment he had told me very proudly: 'I never miss anybody – people miss me'. So I could understand Martin's puzzlement and reservations when he seemed to be asking me in so many ways: 'If it hurts, how can you call it getting better?'

4

On Gang Dynamics

In this chapter I shall try to identify the main characteristics of 'gang dynamics', both in terms of internal and external gang structures, referring only to those aspects of group dynamics that clearly differentiate them from gang dynamics. After presenting some clinical material I will attempt to clarify the post-Kleinian frame of reference I relied upon in my thinking. I will start with a reference to the assessment of an adolescent girl which should help us to focus on some aspects of group dynamics.

Julia

Certain aspects of the first two sessions seem pertinent to my theme. Julia was seventeen but seemed a little older than her age. Her delicate face probably looked particularly pale because of her black jumper and black leather jacket, and she had a very tired expression. As soon as she sat down she told me she had previously attended the Clinic and that she had stopped coming, which she should not have done. She still had plenty of problems; the main one was that she 'did not want to sleep', indeed she had not slept at all for several days. She did not even try to. At most she might lie down for an hour or so.

I asked Julia what she did instead. She said she had a very wide circle of friends; many of them were, like herself, neither working nor at school, so she could see them at all hours of the day and night. It soon became apparent that Julia was not sexually involved with any of her friends and she stressed that she did not seek involvement with anyone, 'just the occasional one-night stand'. She told me how, whenever she joined a group of friends, they would cheer up at her arrival, saying 'Oh here comes crazy Julia'. She was always the clown of the group, making her friends laugh; she felt that she *had* to make them laugh. That was what they really liked about her and why they accepted her.

She looked very depressed when she said this and I felt my heart sinking; I think I was experiencing, in the countertransference, the counterpart of her compulsive cheerfulness. What would happen were she not the 'life and soul of the party', I asked. She felt sure that her friends would not want to have anything to do with her; they only accepted her because she was 'the clown'. Maybe, she said, if they did not laugh at her jokes, they would laugh at her instead. I asked her whether she had had any such experience and she replied, 'Oh yes', this was the reason why she had left school. She felt she did not belong to any group there and that people were often laughing at her. She paused and then said that 'On reflection, this wasn't perhaps always the case', but that she had started missing a lot of school and was eventually expelled. I remarked on the comment, 'this wasn't perhaps always the case', and she seemed intrigued by my suggestion that the perception of outside events could change depending on one's state of mind. There was a very good contact between us and I felt very warm towards Julia in the countertransference. So I was surprised when she looked startled, as if she had been kicked, and said in a rather manic voice that I shouldn't really make such a fuss because she had no serious problem; she was really only worried about what she was going to do that evening, and whether she was going to go to a party. I had the impression at this point that somebody in her mind, maybe a group in her mind, had cracked the whip and said: 'You are slipping. All that matters to you is to have fun and keep us amused. Why are you being soppy talking with this woman?' The manic mood receded considerably towards the end of the session, however, and Julia was able to talk about her fear of depression. Since she had stopped treatment, she told me, she had actually spent many days in bed without being able to get up and it had become apparent that her 'never going to bed' at present was related to her fear that, if she were to let go of her manic defences, she might collapse and not be able to get up.

Between the first and the second session, Julia's mother persuaded her daughter to go with her to her general practitioner and to have some sleeping pills prescribed so that she could get one full night's sleep. Julia arrived at the second session looking very sleepy. Her appearance had also changed. Although it was rather a warm day, she was wearing a big cuddly fluffy woollen jumper which made her look like a large teddy bear. Her hair, which had been pulled into a tight pony tail in the previous session, was now loose on her shoulders and her look much softer. She told me that she had slept for nearly 16 hours on one sleeping tablet and that she was spending considerable periods of time at home. She said that both her parents were being kind, particularly her mother. Her mother was bringing her hot drinks and wanted to be helpful in every possible way. Then Julia expressed the wish that her mother would give her more reason for being angry. In fact there *was* something that Julia was angry about. Mother had spoken with one of the members of the group of young friends, John, and told him that Julia was a little 'dopey' at the moment and needed an eye kept on her. The conversation took place when John had called Julia to tell her about somebody's birthday party, but Julia was asleep. She had profoundly resented this intrusion and said she wished her mother had minded her own business. It was clear, nevertheless, that Julia enjoyed her mother's attention and that she was, to say the least, divided between the wish to stay at home tucked up in bed, and the wish to be always around when a party took place.

I asked her whether she had gone to the birthday party after all. She said that John had offered to come and pick her up. He was one of the few people in the group who had 'got his act together', and was working four days a week in a fast food shop and had saved enough money to buy 'an old banger'. So Julia had gone to the party in the 'old banger' and had been listening to the music lying on a beanbag, because she felt too tired to dance. To her surprise, her friends had been really nice to her; they didn't seem to mind her not being 'the clown'. One of them, Bonnie, had even said, 'Thank God you got yourself some sleep'. Julia had fallen asleep, in spite of the music, and John had woken her up, saying she would be more comfortable sleeping in a bed, and he had taken her back home 'very early' – at 2.00 am in the morning. Julia heard the day after that they had been up all night. But at this point I did not have the feeling that she could not forgive herself for missing out on the rest of the party.

I shall not give an account of the subsequent assessment sessions, or of the treatment that followed them, since I chose this material to focus on the aspects of internal and external group dynamics that differentiate them from 'gang dynamics', the main focus of this paper to which I come now.

We can state that the binding force of a gang is its destructive aim (Rosenfeld, 1971). The gang gets together under the guise of offering protection to its members, but its primary task is to do damage. The group, by contrast, is often permeated by very hurtful dynamics such as making outsiders feel excluded, but it doesn't get together *in order* to hurt.

We can see that Julia's dread of feeling an outsider is clearly present in the description of the school as she perceived it at the outset. 'She did not belong and people were laughing at her.' By the time she told me about it, she was not so sure that this was the case; she was much more worried about being excluded from her current group of friends. Plentiful evidence eventually emerged that her notion of having to remain the clown in order to be accepted was much more closely related to the voice of an internal group, probably performing a defensive function against her dread of depression, than to the external one. The latter turned out to be surprisingly friendly.

John, for example, comes across as a caring older brother who takes seriously Julia's mother's request to look after her. He picks her up from home and he takes her back home. If we look at his function symbolically, we can see him as providing a link between the group structure and the family structure at a time when Julia seems to have a great need to fall back, albeit temporarily, into the fold of the family, but does not want to lose contact with the group. The group and the family do not stand in opposition to one another, and Julia does not lose her membership when she shifts to accepting a more dependent relationship on her mother.

It is significant that, while still a member of the group, Julia is able to refer herself to the Tavistock and to resume treatment. The gang, by contrast, is intrinsically *anti-parental* in quality. It may also perform a surveillance function. For instance, another adolescent patient referred to the Clinic for persistent nightmares belonged to a gang which only allowed him to attend treatment on condition that he reported on each session in detail. Fortunately this interference could be dealt with in the treatment.

The Gang Structure

Some aspects of my work with a patient might help to clarify the gang's characteristic mode of functioning. I saw Pekka three times a week for nearly five years from the age of eighteen. I will focus in particular on some of his dream material, and on its transference significance, during the first three years of treatment.

Pekka is the first child of a Finnish couple living in London. He has a sister eighteen months younger and a brother four years his junior. His mother was very depressed after his birth and he was looked after a great deal by his maternal grandmother. He was breast-fed, he thinks, only for a few days. He doesn't remember ever feeling close either to mother or father but had a better relationship with his sister. It was his sister, Ulla, who told him that he had always been very attacking of his baby brother Eric, who was breastfed by mother for some months.

Pekka could not be left alone in a room with Eric, but he didn't know what they feared he might do. He does remember having fierce fights with Eric when they were older and that on one occasion he attempted to strangle him.

Pekka had always been successful in his studies, triumphing over his siblings, in particular Eric, whom he described as a total academic failure. He sought treatment on account of severe migraines which had been extensively and inconclusively investigated from the neurological point of view. At times the migraines were so acute that he had to spend the day in bed. When he started treatment he was involved in a tormenting homosexual relationship with a boy of his age, Gordon. He had previously had two sexual relationships with girls, and when he spoke about his heterosexual relationships I was confronted with a picture of such intense sadomasochism that I felt they were much more troubled than his homosexual ones. Pekka's relationship with his current boyfriend Gordon will give us opportunity to think about an external gang (albeit only a gang of two) in Pekka's life.

I would like first to focus on material that will enable us to identify the main characteristics of Pekka's internal gang. Only two weeks after starting treatment he brought me a very significant dream.

> He was with a group of men involved in extracting a bomb from a long, metal shaft. Pekka became very frightened, he felt like running away but was firmly held back by the leader of the group, who said 'Now you are involved in it and you are going to stay.' Pekka found himself unable to disobey or question this injunction. He carried on with the extraction of the bomb. He then found himself with the same 'group' (or should we say gang) in an airport where they were supposed to plant the bomb. They put it under a counter; explosion was imminent. As they were making their getaway, Pekka looked at the people in the airport, anticipating the sight of them as corpses when the bomb had exploded.

This dream puts across very vividly the tightness of the gang structure and Pekka's masochistic submission to the ring-leader, a destructive part of his personality. We were to meet it in many other dreams and repeatedly saw it at work in the sabotaging of the analytic relationship. It is certainly significant that the dream took place so close to the beginning of treatment: a sort of warning there was *no* way out.

Pekka's main motivation for seeking help, as I have said, was his hope of being relieved of his excruciating migraines. He perceived no conscious discomfort about his external relationships, nor had he, when I first met him, a notion of internal relationships. The dream suggests, nevertheless, that his seeking analytic help threatened the absolute power of the internal gang. Such power had to be strongly reaffirmed; the voice that asks for release from the murderous mission comes across as a hopeless whimper, but the internal structures guarding the 'status quo' speak with the thundering voice of the ringleader.

You Are In It and Here You Are Going to Stay

It was clear that neither Pekka nor I should believe that one can give up membership of the Mafia just by saying, 'I am frightened, I want to get away'. Godfathers are not well known for their compassionate and tender feelings. Pekka submits. It is indeed interesting to see how his masochistic knuckling under is immediately followed by an identification with the killers, a flipping over into sadism. So when Pekka described observing the people in the airport and imagining them as corpses, there was a chilling ring of 'mission accomplished' in his voice.

The horror was projected into me, and the submission to the ring-leader seemed to involve a commitment to mass murder. Pekka initially acted out the mission of attacking himself and me, as a parental object, in his external life in the highly sadomasochistic relationship with his boyfriend. In that relationship he was repeatedly putting his own safety, at times even his own life, at risk. I shall return to this theme later.

My interpretation of the 'airport dream', as we came to call it during the analysis, in terms of an attack on 'mother's babies', was somehow brushed aside by Pekka at a conscious level. In the countertransference I perceived an undermining of my attempts to formulate (generate) anything that could make emotional sense and provide a useful link with the 'here-and-now'. Interestingly, the theme always became more explicit in the dream life. Pekka dreamt of running over his brother in his car, and it was on this occasion that he told me about having actually tried to strangle his brother in one of their many fights. Indeed, for some time in his dream life a dialogue seemed to take place between me and a part of Pekka that wished to get out of the gang. His dreams often seemed to be related to a recent interpretation and to bring the work forward. However, at a conscious level there was, for a long time, a total denial of psychic reality. Pekka was indeed puzzled about the recurrence of certain themes, but felt sufficiently emotionally detached to give me very *free* associations. For instance, after one of the many 'baby killing' dreams, including one where he fired his sister through the mouth of a cannon, he told me that when he met a pregnant woman he often thought of the 'Sharon Tate murder'. *Emotionality* and *meaning* were both victims of this inner holocaust.

I have mentioned the recurrence of some themes in Pekka's dreams, and will quote just one of the many that bear a similarity to the airport dream. It occurred about 18 months after the beginning of treatment, when Pekka had partly disengaged himself from 'the mission' of the gang and there was some evidence of attachment to me in the transference. He dreamt of being with a friend called Peter (Pekka is the Finnish equivalent of Peter). They were approached by two men who looked like Iranian fundamentalists, and who took Peter away. He didn't show any resistance, and they then took him to see the corpse of his friend, which was going to be buried under the tarmac. They told him he had been killed because 'he had exposed himself to dangerous Western influences.' Intimidating dreams such as this one frightened Pekka away from my 'dangerous influence' and drew him back into submission to the gang's tyranny.

Such antidevelopmental shifts were paralleled, in external life, by a tightening of the sadomasochistic relationship with Gordon: a return into the fold of the 'gang of two'. When Pekka was drawn back into the structure of the internal gang, he also submitted masochistically to Gordon, just as he had submitted to the ringleader in the 'dream of the airport'. He agreed to accompany Gordon on the big dipper in a funfair on a day when his migraine was so painful that he could have cried but didn't. 'If I complain, he'll tighten the screws. He tells me I am a wimp. He tells me I have got the feelings of a woman.' But the coin could flip and Pekka could become quite merciless with Gordon. On one occasion, for instance, after seeing the film *Prick Up Your Ears*, Gordon had become very anxious. In the film the writer Joe Orton is killed with a hammer by his boyfriend while he is asleep. Gordon then couldn't sleep or, when he did sleep, had terrible nightmares, and Pekka treated him sadistically with mockery and contempt, reducing him to tears. Since the essence of the gang's mission is the killing and tormenting of mother's child, it does *not* matter which child is being tormented. The phantasy can thus be acted out in both sadistic and masochistic roles.

Pekka often felt persecuted; the police were after him in dream after dream. In one of them he was being chased and was running on thin ice, in danger of falling into the dark and murky water. He could see little hands through the cracks in the ice – tiny 'babies' hands'. He was very frightened when he told me about this dream and, when he left, he said 'See you tomorrow' although there was a weekend interval before the next session. In the Monday session he brought me the first dream in which he was clearly asking me for protection against his persecutors:

> He was on the couch and I was sitting behind him – rats were coming out from the side of the couch. He was wearing shorts and had sunflower seeds on his legs – the rats were making for the sunflower seeds and would have bitten him. I got up and lashed the rats to death.

Gradually a wish to be rescued began to emerge. For the first time, Pekka referred to his relationship with Gordon as sordid and repugnant. The sunflower seeds in the dream strike me as a very complex symbol. At first I thought they might be a reference to squandering of seminal fluid; subsequent material, however, suggests that they might symbolise true seeds, the *potentialities* of Pekka's capacity to emerge from the darkness of the gang structure and turn towards the sun, as sunflowers do. Later in our work, the sun did come to be very clearly related to the frightening intensity of close relationships. His anxiety about getting sunburned was objective but also connected with his fear of close relationships.

After the summer break, in the third year of treatment, I had returned from my holiday very suntanned. Pekka remarked on it and said I had certainly been abroad because there had not been much sunshine in England, 'unless', he said, 'you have discovered a sunny spot over here, but you don't tell us about it!' He seemed to perceive himself as 'out there', in the cold, just one of the patients, one of the children. Then, shortly afterwards, he had a dream about a suntanned couple.

> He was travelling in Turkey, alone on his bike. In a very beautiful place, probably Ephesus, he met a man and woman who looked full of life and interests and seemed very close to one another. They were a middle-aged couple, both very suntanned, and they were kind to him; he visited the sites with them. Then the couple left and he was alone with his bike.

It looks, in the dream, as if the couple is withdrawing into the intimacy of a close relationship, leaving him alone, all by himself, a boy alone with his bike. He himself had no doubt that the dream was related to my holiday and my suntan. He can never expose himself to the sun, he said: he burns easily, while I have obviously got the sort of skin that can soak up the sun.

By this time the gang structure had considerably lost its grip on Pekka. He had tried to rekindle the moribund relationship with Gordon during my holiday but it had lost all its glamour. He had been exposed, like never before, to the pain of separation, to the feeling of exclusion from the parental 'close relationship', the 'secret place I don't tell my patients about'. However, the reference to Ephesus seems to hint at the notion that he might be confronted with a *mystery* rather than a *secret*. This material gives an indication of the psychic pain Pekka had avoided by means of the protection of his internal gang. A fluctuation between allegiance to narcissistic structures and attempts to sustain object relationships has permeated the work of the first two years.

Theoretical Frame of Reference

To return to the main focus of this paper, I would like to clarify the theoretical frame of reference that helped me formulate and give substance to a hypothesis about 'gang dynamics'.

The first reference to a beckoning from destructive parts of the personality is to be found in Freud's case history of 'The Ratman' (1909), in which he describes the patient being given injunctions to commit a crime by internal voices he refers to as 'agents provocateurs'. In the same case history, Freud refers to the patient's personality as being split into three very different characters. Much later, in 'Splitting of the Ego in the Process of Defence' (1938), Freud will return to this seminal concept, but with no emphasis on the destructive parts of the personality.

This issue is not developed by Klein until very late in her writings. 'On the Development of Mental Functioning' (1958) clearly identifies destructive parts of the self as being different from the superego. This represented a turning point in her theory since she had previously seen the destructive aspects of the personality as embedded in the harshness of the superego. In the 1958 paper, she formulates the hypothesis that these parts exist in a separate area of the mind, in the deep unconscious, and that they are split off from the ego and the superego, remaining unintegrated and unmodified by a normal process of growth. Actually she puts forward the rather pessimistic view that there might be destructive aspects of the personality that cannot ever be totally integrated, even in a long analytical process.

The concept of splitting between parts of the personality is central to the post-Kleinian theoretical development drawn upon as a frame of reference throughout this chapter. In 'Terror, Persecution and Dread', Donald Meltzer writes:

Where dependence on internal good objects is rendered unfeasible by damaging masturbatory attacks and when dependence on a good external object is unavailable or not acknowledged, the addictive relationship to a bad part of the self, the submission to tyranny, takes place. An illusion of safety is promulgated by the omniscience of the destructive part. (1979, p. 105)

Herbert Rosenfeld describes this 'destructive part' as an internal 'gang' in 'A clinical approach to the psychoanalytic theory of the life and death instincts: an investigation into the aggressive aspects of narcissism' (1971). There he says, referring to patients strikingly reminiscent of Pekka:

The destructive narcissism of these patients appears often highly organised, as if one were dealing with a powerful gang, dominated by a leader, who controls all the members of the gang to see that they support one another in making the criminal destructive work more effective and powerful. (1971, p. 174)

Rosenfeld stresses that the essence of the gang formation is to join forces in order to perform 'criminal destructive work'; he highlights the tight grip it holds on other parts of the personality in order to maintain the 'status quo':

The narcissistic organisation ... has a defensive purpose to keep itself in power and so maintain the 'status quo'. The main aim seems to be to prevent the weakening of the organisation and to control the members of the gang so that they will not desert the destructive organisation and join the positive parts of the self or betray the secrets of the gang to the police, the protective superego, standing for the helpful analyst who might be able to save the patient. (1971, p. 174)

We have a striking example of a powerful internal gang dominated by a leader in the first dream Pekka brought to his therapy. He was asking permission – albeit in a very weak voice, as yet – to disengage himself from a deadly mission, but he was told, in no uncertain terms, by the ringleader, 'You are in it and here you are going to stay'. In Rosenfeld's words, members of the gang must 'support one another in making the criminal destructive work more effective and powerful'. Although Pekka is not himself a victim of the mass murder in the airport mission, some aspects of the dream point clearly to dangers to his life. The dark shaft from which the bomb needs to be extracted seems a very apt representation of the rectum and subsequent material gave me plentiful evidence of Pekka's dread of contracting Aids through anal intercourse, as well as a terror of being imprisoned in a lethal, dark 'claustrum' (Meltzer, 1982).

It is true that for a long period of treatment, Pekka did not ask me explicitly to provide reinforcements for the life-supporting parts of himself which were caught in the addictive grip of 'the gang'. Instead, he was devoted to the murderous mission, even though he might become one of the victims. His wish to be rescued emerged gradually and the first hopeful dream, in this respect, was the one in which I was delivering him from the attacks of the rats.

The addictive quality of gang dynamics also seems to me central, and it is stressed by many authors. For example, Joseph says:

> Such patients feel in thrall to a part of the self that dominates and imprisons them and will not let them escape, even though they feel life beckoning outside ... [the patient] is not only dominated by an aggressive part of himself, but ... this part is actively sadistic towards another part of the self that is masochistically caught up in this process and ... this has become an addiction. (1982, p. 451)

Steiner suggests that:

> It is misleading to view this as an innocent part of the self caught in the grip of malevolent organisation, instead I will try to show that a perverse relationship may exist and the healthy part of the self may collude and allow itself to be knowingly taken over by the narcissistic gang. (1982, pp. 242-3)

As I said earlier when I touched briefly upon Pekka's reaction to my summer holiday during the third year of treatment, it would be beyond the scope of this chapter to describe in any detail the type of anxieties and the new gathering of defences that emerged when the gang structure began to loosen its grip on Pekka. I would like to conclude by remarking that subsequent developments made it increasingly clear that the 'illusion of safety promulgated by the omniscience of the destructive part' (Meltzer, 1967) was, in the first instance, a promise of protection from persecutory anxieties. These were in fact continuously intensified and increased by the addiction to sadomasochistic phantasies; acting in the transference; and acting out. With the gradual relinquishment of this addiction the persecutory anxieties receded, to be replaced by painful reactions to separation and feelings of despair about reparation being impossible. Indeed, it became apparent that Pekka abandoned object relationships and took refuge in a narcissistic structure because he could not bear depressive anxieties which perhaps did not find sufficient containment in his earliest childhood.

The voice of the Godfather owes its main irresistible attractiveness to the ruthless, unthinking slogans of the gang that say that there is nothing sacred, nothing precious, nothing that is worth shedding tears about.[1] When these slogans begin to be perceived as the quintessence of lies, the path to thinking and seeking of truth is open. The path is also then open to a psychic pain that I shall describe in the beautiful words of Keats:

> Where but to think
> is to be full of sorrow
> and leaden-eyed despair.

[1] I have had many enriching discussions on the subject of gangs and gang dynamics with Margot Waddell (cf. Waddell and Williams, 1991).

5

Self-Esteem and Object Esteem

In this chapter I will explore the link between self-esteem and object esteem. I will refer to the concept of self-esteem in Freud's clinical work, and in the metapsychological paper 'Mourning and Melancholia' (1917), which I see as a most significant watershed in relation to this concept. My own suggestion is that the term 'object esteem' is intrinsically inherent to the new perspective on self-esteem opened up by Freud in 'Mourning and Melancholia', and I will attempt to link my thoughts on this issue with some clinical material.

The Shift in the Concept of Self-Esteem

In following the references to the concept of self-esteem in Freud's work I find a marked contrast between his technique in the clinical work and the theoretical formulations of 'Mourning and Melancholia'. This is not surprising, for all Freud's major clinical papers were written before 1915, the year in which he wrote 'Mourning and Melancholia'. Here I include the Wolfman too, because although this paper was not published until 1918, it was actually written in 1914. Indeed, perhaps it is only in the work of Ruth Mack Brunswick (1928), who analysed the Wolfman in 1926-27 and who was undoubtedly deeply influenced by Freud's teaching, subsequent to the watershed of 'Mourning and Melancholia', that we find an analytic approach and a technique more congruous with the concepts formulated in that paper.

I will focus initially on the clinical paper that provides the most interesting references to the concept of self-esteem, i.e. the 'Ratman', a case study I referred to also in Chapter 4. At the beginning of treatment, Freud asked the patient to say 'everything that came into his head, even if it was unpleasant to him or seemed unimportant or irrelevant or senseless' and 'gave him leave to start his communications with any subject he pleased'. Freud's account begins as follows:

He had a friend, he told me, of whom he had an extraordinarily high opinion. He used always to go to him when he was tormented by some criminal impulse, and ask him whether he despised him as a criminal. His friend used then to give him moral support by assuring him that he was a man of irreproachable conduct, and had probably been in the habit, from his youth onwards, of taking a dark view of his own life.

At an earlier date, he went on, another person had exercised a similar influence over him. This was a nineteen year old student (he himself had been fourteen or fifteen at the time) who had taken a liking to him, and had raised his *self-esteem* [my italics] to an extraordinary degree, so that he appeared to himself to be a genius. This student had subsequently become his tutor, and had suddenly altered his behaviour and begun treating him as though he were an idiot. At length he had noticed that the student was interested in one of his sisters, and had realised that he had only taken him up in order to gain admission into the house. This had been the first great blow of his life. (1909, p. 160)

Freud obviously took this communication very seriously. It immediately followed his request for the patient to free associate, and he probably considered this blow to the Ratman's self-esteem as one of the important causative factors of his illness. It is confirmed by the fact that we often find Freud reassuring the Ratman in a way that might not have been unlike the reassurances of the friend who 'assured him he was a man of irreproachable conduct'. We hear Freud, for instance, saying 'in the further course of our conversation I pointed out to him that he ought logically to consider himself as in no way responsible for any of these traits in his character, for all of these reprehensible impulses originated from his infancy, and were only derivatives of his infantile character surviving in his unconscious; and he must know that moral responsibility could not be applied to children' (p. 185). Or, 'I said a word or two upon the good opinion I had formed of him and this gave him visible pleasure' (p. 178). It seems significant to me that, in working with the Ratman, Freud frequently stresses the split between conscious and unconscious, adult and infantile in order to exempt his patient from any responsibility or feelings of guilt. Even so, in the case history Freud clearly mentions a conflict between love and hate, and refers to destructive aspects of the personality. I will quote some examples:

A battle between love and hate was raging in the lover's breast, and the object of both these feelings was one and the same person. (p. 191)

At some prehistoric period in his childhood he had been seized with fury (which had subsequently become latent) against the father whom he loved so much. (pp. 207-208)

The reference to a 'prehistoric period of childhood' is interesting in this context as Freud is obviously referring here to very early feelings. Elsewhere in the same paper he also uses the word 'archaic'.

Freud then poses the following question: 'It might be asked why this intense love of his had not succeeded in extinguishing his hatred, as usually happens when there are two opposing impulses. We could only presume that the hatred must flow from some source, must be connected with some particular cause, which made it indestructible' (p. 181). The answer to this question is given about sixty pages into the case history:

> The love had not succeeded in extinguishing the hatred but only in driving it down into the unconscious, and in the unconscious the hatred, safe from the danger of being destroyed by the operations of consciousness, is able to persist and even to grow ... The necessary condition for the occurrence of such a strange state of affairs in a person's erotic life appears to be that at a very early age, somewhere again in the *prehistoric* [my italics] period of his infancy, the two opposites should have been split apart and one of them, usually the hatred, has been repressed. (p. 239)

A particularly striking statement follows on the next page:

> We may suppose, then, that in the cases of unconscious hatred with which we are concerned, the sadistic components of love have, from *constitutional* [my italics] causes, been exceptionally strongly developed, and have consequently undergone a premature and all too thorough suppression, and that the neurotic phenomena we have observed arise, on the one hand, from conscious feelings of affection which have become exaggerated as a reaction, and, on the other hand, from sadism persisting in the unconscious in the form of hatred. (p. 240)

The reference to *constitutional* causes sounds like an anticipation of the concept of primary sadism in Melanie Klein.

More references to hatred and destructiveness, linking Freud's work with Abraham's and Klein's and that of many post-Kleinian analysts, are to be found in the Ratman than in 'Beyond the Pleasure Principle' (1920), so frequently quoted. In 1920 Freud was to talk for the first time about the separate instincts as Eros and Thanatos, and here his approach to states of mind is predominantly biological; in fact the entropy theory – the tendency for the libido to return to the inanimate state, to death – has really very little to do with emotions and object relations. For this reason, I find the frequent references to 'Beyond the Pleasure Principle' made by Melanie Klein in order to establish a continuity between Freud's theory and her own not very convincing. In my opinion the link is much more to be found in Freud's clinical writings, and the Ratman in particular. It is mainly in the 'Original Record of the Case', containing Freud's day-by-day notes on the patient, that we find examples of the extreme destructiveness of the patient's unconscious phantasies and dreams. I should like to quote some of them:

> It was a question of a picture of me [Freud] and my wife in bed with a dead child lying between us. He (the patient) knew the origin of this. When he was a little boy, age uncertain, perhaps five or six, he was lying between his father and mother and wetted the bed, upon which his father beat him and turned him out. The dead child can only be his sister Katherine. He must have gained by her death. The scene occurred, as he confirmed, after her death. (p. 284)

The vividness of the transference is also very clearly expressed in the following description: 'His demeanour during all this was that of man in desperation and one who was trying to save himself from blows of terrific violence; he buried his head in his hands, rushed away, covered his face with his arm, etc. He told me that his father had a passionate temper, and then did not know what he was doing' (p. 284). This seems to be a clear reference to the fear of being punished by the father, whose child the patient had wished dead and who had actually died (his sister Katherine).

At the patient's next session, Freud's mother 'was standing in despair while all her children were being hanged. He reminded me of his father's prophecy that he would be a great criminal' (p. 284). The Ratman then proceeded to a direct attack on Freud: he said he knew that a brother of Freud had committed a murder in Budapest and been executed for it. The murder that is split off and projected onto Freud's brother might well be linked with an aspect of the Ratman towards which Freud appears particularly lenient: for example, when the patient describes the suicide of a young dressmaker and considers it a probable consequence of his ruthless behaviour towards her. We could formulate the hypothesis that in this instance, as well, Freud interprets the rather detached and cynical stance of his patient, his total absence of guilt feelings, as related to the fact that this event belonged to the part of his personality which 'contained all his passionate and evil impulses' and which Freud sees as split off from the rest of the Ratman's personality. Again Freud's message seems to be: 'You are not responsible for the misbehaviour of your unconscious.'

Freud likewise seems to see the Ratman purely as a victim of the 'commands' he receives. To quote from Meltzer's *The Kleinian Development* (Meltzer, 1978, pp. 59-60), 'Some of these [commands] were dangerously destructive, such as the command to cut his own throat, or the command to kill the old woman. My impression', says Meltzer, 'is (though Freud does not state it explicitly) that he thinks these commands come from a deeply unconscious and very brutal part of the Ratman's personality, and are directed to one of the two pre-conscious personalities: namely to the infantile polymorphously perverse part.'

Links Between the Ratman and 'Mourning and Melancholia'

I should now like to make some links between the Ratman and 'Mourning and Melancholia'. It is legitimate, I think, to make a connection between these two works because Freud repeatedly stresses the significant links between melancholia or pathological depression, and obsessional neurosis (cf. p. 258), and because the problem of mourning is central to the Ratman's case. Indeed Freud says that he 'regarded the Ratman's sorrow at his father's death as the chief source of the intensity of his illness. His sorrow had found, as it were, a pathological expression in his illness. Whereas, I told him, a normal period of mourning would last from one to two years, a *pathological* [my italics] one like this would last indefinitely' (p. 186).

In 'Mourning and Melancholia' we find a description of the melancholic patient that is in some respect reminiscent of the Ratman. 'The patient represents his ego to us as worthless, incapable of any achievement and morally despicable; he reproaches himself, vilifies himself and expects to be cast out and punished. He abases himself before everyone for being so unworthy' (1917, p. 246). We can now listen to the Ratman talking to Freud very much on these lines:

> Things soon reached a point at which, in his dream, his waking phantasies, and his associations, he began heaping the grossest and filthiest abuse upon me and my family, though in his deliberate actions he never treated me with anything but the greatest respect. His demeanour as he repeated his insults to me was that of a man in despair. 'How can a gentleman like you, Sir', he used to ask, 'let yourself be abused in this way by a low, good-for-nothing fellow like me? You ought to turn me out: that's all I deserve'. (1909, p. 209)

Freud repeatedly used reassurance in the treatment of the Ratman, but he expressed very negative views on this technique in 'Mourning and Melancholia':

> It would be equally fruitless from a *scientific* and a *therapeutic* point of view to contradict a patient who brings these accusations against this ego. He must surely be right in some way and be describing something that is as it seems to him to be true. Indeed, we must at once confirm some of his statements without reservation. He really is as lacking in interest and as incapable of love and achievement as he says. He also seems to us justified in certain other self-accusations; it is merely that he has a keener eye for the truth than other people who are not melancholic. When in his heightened self-criticism he describes himself as petty, egotistic, dishonest, lacking in independence, one whose sole aim has been to hide the weakness of his own nature, it may be, so far as we know, that he has come pretty near to understanding himself; we only wonder why a man has to be ill before he can be accessible to a truth of this kind. (1917, p. 246)

On the other hand, as Meltzer points out (1979), Freud opens up a fundamental question in his paper: 'Whose pain is it really? Is the patient really in pain?' The answer to this question is given by Freud in the following:

> If one listens patiently to a melancholic's many and various self-accusations, one cannot in the end avoid the impression that often the most violent of them are hardly at all applicable to the patient himself, but that with insignificant modifications they do fit someone else, someone whom the patient loves or has loved or should love. Every time one examines the facts this conjecture is confirmed. So we find the key to the clinical picture as we perceive that the self-reproach is a reproach against the loved object which has been shifted away from it, onto the patient's own ego. (1917, p. 248)
> If the love for the object – a love which cannot be given up though the object is given up – takes refuge in narcissistic identification, then the hate comes into operation on this substitutive object, abusing it, debasing it, making it suffer and deriving sadistic satisfaction from it suffering. The self-tormenting in melancholia, *which is without doubt enjoyable*, signifies, just like the corresponding phenomenon in obsessional neurosis, a satisfaction of trends of sadism and hate which relate to an object, and which have been turned round upon the subject's own self in the ways we have been discussing. In both disorders (and this is where we can see the pertinence of the reference in the Ratman) the patients usually still succeed, by a circuitous path of self-punishment, in taking revenge on the original object and in tormenting their loved one through their illness, having resorted to it in order to avoid the need to express their hostility to him openly. (1917, p. 251)

We could not imagine that by this time Freud would have found it helpful to console the Ratman by telling him that he had formed a very good opinion of him, or that he was in no way responsible for his attacks on his objects. Although the main reference in 'Mourning and Melancholia' appears to be to external objects, one can feel that he is on the threshold of the formulation that was to take shape in the Structural Theory (Freud, 1923), and that what he says about the melancholic is not far removed from a reference to identification with *internal* objects that occupy an *internal* space. It is particularly clear in the very beautiful passage where Freud describes 'the shadow of the object falling upon the ego' (p. 249) in this type of identification.

In the work of Karl Abraham, which deepens in particular Freud's insight in terms of the definition of mania, we find an unmistakable reference to internal objects: we also find that Abraham views patients full of self-reproach and who display marked feelings of inadequacy as 'incapable of loving' (1911-16) and always identified with battered internal objects (1924) – his clinical technique is not based on reassurance, but on enhancing a reparation of the internal world in order to bring about an identification with a loved object, rather than with a debased and hated one. One such example is particularly significant in relation to Freud's remark about the 'shadow of the object falling upon the ego'. Abraham tells us about a patient who has been able to introject a loved mother very firmly. He refers in this context to Freud's 1917 paper and says: 'We have only to reverse his statement that "the shadow of the lost object falls upon the ego" and say that in this case, it was not the shadow, but the bright radiance of his loved mother which was shed upon her son' (1924). Melanie Klein was influenced by Freud's theoretical formulations and greatly influenced by Abraham's. Her theory of early development, in particular her reference to *primary sadism and envy*, not seen just as a response to external frustrations or 'narcissistic blows', provides a much clearer frame of reference for the shift in technique that Freud advocated in 'Mourning and Melancholia'. There he defined an approach based on reassurance and exempting a patient from responsibility as 'fruitless both from a scientific and a therapeutic point of view'. As I suggested earlier, this might be his retrospective self-criticism of the technique he used in treating patients like the Ratman. On the basis of Klein's theory, this approach would deprive the patient of insight into *his* contribution to the quality of his internal world, and therefore of the hope of an improvement in its quality. (Indeed, hopefulness does not loom large in the Ratman's case.) Klein sees this process as taking place through a gradual sparing of internal objects from the attacks of the destructive parts of the personality, as it is sustained by the therapeutic alliance. And in *Envy and Gratitude* (1957, p. 188), she says that through this process 'a good object is established who loves and protects the self and is loved and protected by the self. This is the basis for trust in one's own goodness.' The quotation seems to me to shed great light on the link between self-esteem and 'object esteem'.

Clinical Material

I would like to expand on this theoretical exposition by describing some of my work with a patient whose poor self-esteem clearly mirrored a very poor 'object esteem'. Ingrid was in her late 30s and had two adolescent daughters. I started seeing her twice weekly and subsequently increased her sessions to three. Her daughters were also seen intensively in the Tavistock Clinic Adolescent Department. Aspects of the patient's history can help one to understand the lack of internalisation of a beautiful loved object that could 'shed a bright radiance' on her perception of herself. The experience she described in the early days of our work as a feeling of 'never knowing where home is' opened her to offers of a 'home' from most doubtful sources, and made her prone to form abusive internal and external alliances. A very precarious object relationship impregnated by very denigratory and hostile feelings brought Ingrid to establish a 'narcissistic object relationship' (Rosenfeld, 1971) with parts of herself, often destructive parts of the self. This narcissistic organisation had in turn made her object relations ever more precarious, and a vicious circle had become established.

Ingrid's parents, who are both Norwegian, had travelled a great deal throughout her childhood because of her father's business. The patient described her mother as 'extremely beautiful, but very glacial' and her father as a cultured man, very passionate and knowledgeable about art. Ingrid spent a great deal of her early childhood away from her parents: in her third or fourth month of life there was a separation for some weeks, and for a number of months she was in the care of a nanny; she was sent to boarding school at the age of six. Two sisters were born, one when she was four, the other when she was nine and already at boarding school; she knows that she wet her bed at boarding school but she doesn't remember crying, and she said she soon learned to 'keep a stiff upper lip'.

The patient referred her two adolescent daughters to the Clinic, saying that she had difficulties with both of them because they didn't respect her authority at all and treated her with utter contempt. She had by then been divorced from their father for many years. It became clear during the diagnostic interviews that one could only help the adolescent daughters if the mother was also helped herself, as it was apparent that she was opening herself to her daughters' contemptuous attitude. Masochistic aspects of her character were much in evidence during the assessment, which was, incidentally, not carried out by me.

In one of the first sessions Ingrid told me that she was a 'specialist in failures'. She had done very badly in her studies and knew that her parents had been very disappointed over it; in particular, she had abandoned the study of a musical instrument, which she felt to be a very direct attack on her father and his love for music. Indeed it might be important to mention how she interrupted her studies. During the Easter holidays when she was eighteen, and staying with her parents, she made a serious suicide attempt by taking barbiturates; after a stay in hospital she was admitted for two months to a psychiatric nursing home. Ingrid then did not resume any type of study for many years. In her early thirties she enrolled at university to read archaeology but dropped out after one year. She told me that she made her tutor feel very hopeless and helpless, and described with an element of triumph the many failed attempts that this tutor and a number of friends had made to convince her to resume her studies.

Ingrid had met her first husband, an Englishman, in Norway and had then moved to England after marrying him. She told me that she had been treated by him, and subsequent men in her life, in a rather brutal way, but that she might have somehow asked for it. 'I'm like those dogs who lie on their backs asking to be kicked', she said. Ingrid had also had two attempts at therapy prior to the beginning of her treatment with me, and described with some satisfaction how they had both failed miserably and how she stopped them both very abruptly. Not surprisingly, Ingrid did not envisage a much better prognosis for our work. She told me in one of the very early sessions, 'If I can put up enough resistance, you will have no power against my determination to be unmovable.'

While the tenacity of the 'narcissistic organisation' (Steiner, 1987) loomed large, the tenuousness of object relationship was apparent in the feeling of precariousness Ingrid experienced in the relationship with me. Arriving for her third session, when I was still seeing her twice a week, and just after our first weekend break, her watch was five minutes fast and she thought I was late. When I rang the receptionist at the time of her session, Ingrid was standing ready to leave as she thought I had forgotten about her session. She also told me at the beginning of her treatment that she was worried I might suddenly do something absolutely unexpected, for instance, sit in a different place or talk with a different voice. The beginning of our work was therefore characterised by projections of a feeling of precariousness into me. Ingrid literally, on some occasions, had one foot in and one foot out as she lay on the couch, with on occasions during part of the session, one foot on the floor.

At this early stage, Ingrid often reproached me for depriving her of a feeling of 'being special', which she said had been enhanced by her two previous therapists. Thus she dreamt of being an archbishop, or rather, of having put on the clothes of an archbishop; she was preaching in a church, but she had put the clothes on in such a way that they were open at the back and showed her own clothes underneath. Someone sitting behind her, very suggestive of my sitting behind her when she lay on the couch, could see it was 'all a masquerade' (her own words).

In fact, Ingrid was pleased when I made a link with something she had told me in a previous session or when I remembered the names of the numerous members of her family, but her pleasure was often obfuscated by the cloud which looms large in a remark such as: 'I feel a sort of cold respect at your brilliance in remembering, at your extraordinary ability to remember, if I were more human I would be grateful for your incredible attentiveness.' The communication is significant in the context of this chapter, for Ingrid's difficulty in tolerating feelings of appreciation in the transference, namely in tolerating 'object esteem', seemed to be mirrored by a feeling of lack of self-esteem: 'If I were more human'.

Feelings of envy seemed to be present, indeed even predominant in the texture of the remark I have quoted. There were indications that Ingrid's difficulties in accepting sustenance and help were often due to a compound of jealousy and envy. It was apparent in the dream that we often referred to again in our work as 'the dream of the Gouda cheese'.

Ingrid was sitting at a table and a woman sitting on her right was giving her a delicious piece of Gouda cheese, and she ate it. Ingrid thought that the woman had made the cheese herself, but was told that the cheese had been produced in a factory that belonged to this woman and her husband. The husband was sitting to the left of Ingrid. At this point she remembered feeling violently sick in the dream.

I wondered about her having so much liked the cheese at first and then having rejected it to the point of being sick, once she knew the husband was associated with the making of this Gouda-goodness.

There is in fact a Dutch cheese called Gouda, but I felt more inclined to see the distortion (good/gouda) as related to my Italian accent, perhaps with a touch of caricature (Ingrid had no doubts that my accent sounds Italian). Ingrid agreed with this interpretation, recalling an old advert which read 'Drinka pinta milka', parodying the Italian accent. More explicit attacks on 'the couple' were present in dreams and in the transference relationship prior to the first summer break; for instance, in one of those dreams Ingrid was seeing a little girl crying and shouting, 'No mummy, don't go away!' The mother was a prostitute and was going to a brothel with a rich Arab; it is unlikely that such a couple 'in the mind' could be of great help and sustenance to Ingrid during the summer holidays. Another dream, that worried me greatly and that took place immediately prior to the summer holidays, involved both Ingrid's daughters, who had come more clearly to represent, in the treatment, parts of herself. (In external reality the relationship with them had considerably improved due to some change in Ingrid, but also to their making good use of their psychotherapies.)

In the dream, Ingrid had gone for a walk through the wharves along the Thames on her own and then suddenly, she saw both girls in the water. In particular she could see Solweig, the younger, covered with 'an indescribably revolting dirt'; her skin was shining with oil and there were bits of garbage in the water and 'probably shit'. Ingrid shouted to both the girls to come out, but she couldn't see the elder, Ulla, so well. Ingrid's comment was very mild, merely: 'It isn't good for you to swim in those murky waters'. She tried to pull out of the water the younger girl, who was closer to the bank. Solweig held her mother's hand, but then she jumped back into the water and 'played the fool'. As the girl was laughing very loudly, Ingrid could see the inside of Solweig's throat covered with a 'terribly greasy substance'. Ingrid then shouted, 'Most of all don't swallow that water', but Ulla was beckoning Solweig away from her. Ingrid perceived horror in the dream and she woke up, horrified.

In fact this element of horror is probably what gave us both most hope in terms of something in her that wished to struggle with the part of herself represented in the dream by the two girls who seemed literally to laugh at the hand that is held out to help them. I think that one can make a further differentiation perhaps, and think of the younger girl as possibly a more accessible child part of Ingrid, as described by Rosenfeld (1971) as enslaved to the tyranny of a destructive part, represented possibly in the dream by the elder daughter who beckoned Solweig back into the murky water.

Indeed, the need to spoil was particularly mobilised in Ingrid when she was exposed to beauty, and it often interfered with her capacity to enjoy beauty in a variety of contexts. Having resumed going to concerts – an activity she had abandoned a long time before – she told me that she had been taken by a sudden impulse to get up and shout in the middle of the performance of a symphony. She wondered how others in the audience could resist the temptation to scream, shout or make a noise that would spoil other people's enjoyment of something so beautiful; yet it was obviously significant that Ingrid could tell me about this phantasy rather than act it out and be forcibly thrown out of the Queen Elizabeth Hall. (The concert was conducted by Claudio Abbado, an Italian conductor.)

I could of course follow many threads in the two-year treatment of this patient, but I shall focus on the problem of self-esteem and object-esteem, and talk about a point in her treatment at which I could see glimpses of her relinquishing certain aspects of this narcissistic organisation. I quote from a period subsequent to our second summer break. Ingrid had turned down an opportunity to spend the holiday in the company of very anti-analytic allies. She told me how in a dream very close to resuming treatment in September, she had dreamt of being in the company of a group of 'friends' and she had heard a child cry. She had run upstairs and picked up the baby – a little girl – in her arms; the baby had stopped crying but Ingrid could still see her lips quivering. She was very frightened that the little girl would start crying again and she very, very gently put her down in her cot, looking at the quivering lip which meant that the baby was going to start crying again. I was particularly struck by the quivering lip in terms of Ingrid's reference to the 'stiff upper lip' of her childhood. Other dreams following that holiday did not tell me about dependent crying babies only. There was, for instance, a reference to an explosion taking place in an Italian village and an old, beautiful villa having been damaged. Ingrid said that the explosion was very reminiscent of the poisonous vapours of Seveso, a village where such vapours had severely damaged a number of people, and she remarked on how much she had been affected by the fact that those vapours were so dangerous, but invisible. The association brought memories of 'horror' when she had heard that a flood in Florence had ruined some works of art in the Uffizi Gallery.

I would now like to conclude this chapter with a dream that Ingrid had at the time of a Christmas break which possibly contained elements of depressive anxiety, and was therefore less worrying than the one of the murky waters. At the beginning of this session, Ingrid had remarked that my voice sounded as if I had a cold (which happened to be true). When I asked her whether this made her think I might be unwell and unable to see her, she said that in her experience, this had happened only once and I had probably to be very ill indeed to cancel sessions with my patients. The dream she told me about involved her mother, whom she had dreamt of more frequently in the past. They were both walking along a beach and the mother was helping Ingrid to reach a place where she might find a bag that she had mislaid; Ingrid associated the bag with one her mother used to have when she was a child. Her mother was carrying by herself a heavy suitcase, the contents of which Ingrid did not know; then her mother fell down on a slimy part of the beach. It was low tide and her clothes got covered with slime, and at this point, Ingrid decided to help her mother carry the heavy suitcase. She felt great relief as it started raining and she saw that the rain was washing the slime off her mother; she also loved the 'warm feeling of the rain on her own face'. This dream seemed to me open to all sorts of interpretation. For instance, the heavy suitcase was very likely to be related to Ingrid's resentment at having recently started full-time work, whereas in the past she had lived on unearned income and was also helped by her first husband. Although she felt I was probably carrying a heavy suitcase, she was not keen to identify with what she called my 'committed way of life'. It certainly also seemed possible to me that the rain in the dream might have something to do with tears, and in this case, I was not thinking only of tears of self-pity, but of tears beginning to hint at depressive anxiety.

However, this work of restoration was in its early stages; it was equivalent perhaps to initial but necessary washing the slime off the damaged painting in the Uffizi Gallery. Much work was to be needed before the 'shadow of the object falling upon the ego' could be replaced in Ingrid by the 'radiance of the object shining upon the ego'.

6

On the Process of Internalisation

Now I will turn to some aspects of the process of internalisation and describe the first two years of work with David, a boy who was eighteen years old when he referred himself to the Tavistock. David was severely disabled, having been born without arms from the elbow down; only after two years of treatment was he able to let go of the grip of his eyes on me and begin to use the couch. I think a description of the development of our relationship during those first two years is pertinent to the theme of this chapter: the beginning of the internalisation of 'an object loves and protects the Self', described by Melanie Klein (1957) as the basic source of inner strength. It is also worth noting that in spite of great privation in his history, David is very different from Martin, whom we met in Chapter 3.

David

David referred himself to the Tavistock Young People's Counselling Service and he knew that the service offered up to four sessions only. He said, on the phone, that a teacher at his college had advised him to get in touch with us because he thought he might have problems and it might be helpful for him to talk to a counsellor. In the telephone call he made no mention of his disability, and he repeated to me, in the first session, that he did not really know why he had decided to ask for an appointment; it had been his tutor's idea. He was attending the first year of an art foundation course and he enjoyed college and enjoyed living in the halls. He launched into a description of his work, and of his painting, but there was no mention of any problem.

He was very articulate, appeared very sure of himself, and put across the feeling he would be very happy if I did not ask any questions. This handsome boy, looking at me with very gripping eyes, was sitting with his stumps held behind the back of the couch, his legs crossed, ear phones around his neck and a walkman clipped to his belt; he was a lively, engaging adolescent, talking about his love of painting. From time to time he would brush his forehead and pull his hair back with his right stump, with a very natural movement, as if passing a hand through his hair. I remember feeling very disconcerted and thinking that we could easily arrive at the end of the session without David making any reference to his disability; I also remember being lost for words.

When I asked David in this first session whether his disability posed any problems with his painting, he smiled with a touch of condescension, a sort of 'here we go again', and answered with very slight annoyance as if I had mentioned something irrelevant. 'You mean the bits missing? That is how I like to call them. You'll be surprised', he said with some pride, 'to hear how much I can do with the little I have got.' Then he told me he went everywhere on his bike, which worked on back pedal brakes, and that he could swim, could cook, wash up, get dressed, could even do up his shirt buttons, do his shopping. He showed me by using a pen how he held his paint brush under his watch strap and moved it with his 'finger' (that is how he referred to a digit in the shape of a Y on the side of his right elbow). He also told me that, for years, he had been practising martial arts and he was a brown belt at karate. The choice of this particular martial art felt all the more puzzling to me when David told me, in this same first session, that he had an artificial foot because he was born with club feet and one had to be amputated when he was twelve. I had noticed a slight limp and a rock in his gait in the corridor as he was walking to my room, but his feet looked quite normal, hidden inside a pair of fashionable trainers.

After I asked him if he had spent long periods in hospital in his childhood, he told me, very casually, that he had several operations on the foot which was later to be amputated. His mother had 'sometimes but not always' been with him in hospital. He remembered very clearly an occasion, he must have been four or five, when Mother was not there. He remembered how, on that occasion, he had given a 'nasty bite' to the hand of the nurse who was trying to give him a pre-med injection and he laughed. He told me that anyhow, he was quite used not to not having Mother around; he had lived in a children's home for nearly seven years.

I was to learn more about David's history in the second session. He had never met his father, who had disappeared at the beginning of Mother's pregnancy; he only knew that he now lived in a foreign country. Mother was only nineteen when he was born, and she lived with her own mother. David was told that Grandmother had not been prepared to look after him when Mother returned to work when he was six months old. 'That's why', he said in a very casual tone of voice, 'I was put in the first children's home'. He did not remember that first one at all, but he remembered the second and the third one well. He also remembered that Mother used to visit him at the weekends and how sometimes she took him for the day to Grandmother's place – but not often, perhaps on his birthdays.

There was a very poignant moment in the second session when David described the colour of the coat Mother used to wear when she visited him at the children's home: it was a sort of peach, or apricot colour. He still remembered the colour very vividly, and I had the impression, as he half-closed his eyes, that he could actually *see* the colour as he was telling me about it. It vividly evoked in my mind the picture of a little boy hanging on with his eyes to the back of Mother's coat as she left, clinging to this visual image, as toddlers might hang on to their mother's coat with their hands.

David also told me that he went to live with Mother when she obtained her own council flat; he was then seven years old. Mother had got married when he was twelve and David now had a half-brother, Colin, who was by this time six years old. 'He has got two feet and two hands', David said about Colin, without my having asked any questions.

In the third session David said that he had found my reference to the many 'bits missing' in his life very interesting. He had never given much of a thought to the seven years in the children's homes, and there might be plenty more that needed attention. Could he come for longer than four sessions? I clarified the brief of the Counselling Service, which offered up to four sessions, but told him that he could refer himself to the Adolescent Department if he wished. I also decided that if he were to do so, I would offer him a vacancy. I started seeing David once a week, and increased his sessions to three per week at the beginning of the second year of treatment. The treatment lasted nearly six years. But I am still convinced that David was only able to call the Tavistock when he first asked for an appointment because of the safe framework of a counselling service that offered a maximum of four sessions. Neither he nor I imagined, when we first met, that we would be working together for a long time.

Very early in the first year of therapy David brought to his session a picture of himself as a baby. He must have been four or five months old, a very beautiful baby sitting on the lap of his very beautiful, very young mother. Retrospectively I think that the transference significance of his bringing me the picture was a wish that I should pretend with him that there had been no children's homes, for he brought me the picture of a family child. It looked as if David was embracing his mother in the picture because his stumps were hidden inside the cardigan she was wearing; Mother's face looked extremely sad.

I described how David kept his stumps behind the back of the couch in the first counselling session and this was to happen many times again. It seemed to be the most comfortable posture for him, and it made him look like a perfectly normal adolescent, just as the baby in the photo looked like a perfectly normal baby. However, I thought that David's mother might already have known that she would have to part from her baby when this photo was taken. Perhaps it was a photo she could look at when he was going to be put in the children's home; perhaps she could only look at him if his stumps were hidden away. Whatever the reality, I was to become very familiar with the picture of a mother who does not want to see the disability, as one of David's internal objects.

I also felt that I was asked, for a long time, to pretend that the disability and the many 'bits missing' in his body and in his life did not exist or, if they existed, that they did not matter. David was cycling to his sessions, about six miles each way in all sorts of weather; he was talking about his twice-weekly karate training and his hopes that he would soon acquire a black belt. He told me, in the casual tone of voice that I had become familiar with from our first meeting, that he was having an affair with a woman nineteen years older than himself, exactly his mother's age. My countertransference was correspondingly very different at the times when David spoke about real achievements, defensive as they might be against feelings of helplessness, from the times when he was swept away in a state of mind of massive projective identification. When David was inside a borrowed identity, I felt that I could not make a real contact with him, and perceived him as extremely elusive. He could probably only tell me about the pain of not being able to take a firm grip on his object by evoking this feeling most powerfully in me. I felt I was presented with an image and that it was difficult, almost impossible, to get in touch with the real David.

A fleeting contact could be established, only to be lost again. The main request that David seemed to put across was not for his needs to be heard, but for the denial of his needs to be admired. Thus, one of the first poems he brought to me, one of the many that were going to be kept in his folder, reads as follows:

I am running now, away from me
Throwing down my role of reality
Becoming a fairy story boy
Where I pulled the sword from the stone
Shook a giant from his throne
Took a princess far from fear
and made the dark sky once more clear.

There does seem to be some insight, in this poem, into the 'shedding of the role of reality', the flight into the projective identification that totally obliterated the disability: a boy with no hands 'pulling the sword from the stone'.

David's transference to me was, initially, very eroticised. In his first therapy session he asked whether it was true that 'patients always fall in love with their analysts'; he had read something about it in a Sunday paper supplement. And when he told me about his impressive achievements, he often spoke in a very seductive tone of voice. The sexual relationship with the older woman, Sonia, had the hallmark of an acting out of Oedipal phantasies. Sonia was married and was having a secret affair with David. He was sure that I was also married; a dream told us that this represented only a small obstacle. About three months after the beginning of treatment, David had a dream in which he came to visit me in my home. I lived in a very beautiful house in Richmond, the rich mound/mountain, the rich place where rich people live, according to David. We were supposed to have a session, but he asked me if he could kiss me and I said he could. I was wearing a silk dressing gown, and it felt very intimate. Then my husband returned home with our two children. David told me where to hide and I obeyed. He then spoke with my husband and explained that we were having a session and he should not really meet people from my family, as he was a patient. My husband went quietly upstairs with the children.

One can hardly think of the father in this dream as a paternal figure. He is more like an accommodating child kept out of the parental bedroom by a rather feeble excuse. David had totally taken over the identity of my husband. This was in fact a very striking dream about the state of mind of projective identification, a defence still desperately needed by David. It was beginning to be very clear to me that his seductiveness, his phantasies of taking a grip on a maternal object, through kissing or intercourse, were not only to be understood as an adolescent revival of powerful genital Oedipal feelings, but also as a massive defence against the anxiety of not having any firm hold on an internal mother, even less so on reliable internal parents. Indeed I had heard in one of the counselling sessions about a recurrent dream David used to have as a child: he was on Mother's lap, sliding down, not able to hold on; there was no mention of Mother holding on to him.

I was aware that my offer of an increase in the number of sessions could be misinterpreted by David as evidence of my having been successfully seduced by him. At the same time I did not feel that it would be possible to help him emerge from the defensive eroticised transference, and all its accompanying excitement, in one weekly session. So I decided to take the risk and after some initial reluctance David started attending three times a week. It is certainly meaningful that it was at this time that he totally disengaged himself from the sexual relationship with Sonia. However, David also spoke very openly about his worry that he might get too used to his sessions by coming more frequently. He seemed intrigued when I said that I must take his need very seriously as I did not feel that there was, at the time, a parent in his mind who performed that function.

There was a dream, very close to the increase in the number of sessions, that pointed to an escalation in the feelings of omnipotence. This dream followed David's visit, at the weekend, to a friend, Kevin, who lived with his parents on a farm. David dreamt that Kevin's father was asking him if he would like to enter into a partnership. In other words, he was offered the co-ownership of a farm. (It happened to be a dairy farm.) Apparently Kevin's father had expressed great admiration for David's achievements during David's visit at the weekend. David was slightly embarrassed when he told me about this dream, because he was beginning to recognise omnipotent identifications when they were very glaring. He went on to say that perhaps I was going to tell him that he intended to enter into partnership with Mr Tavistock; he could see without much difficulty how related this dream was to the greater access he had been given to my time.

Although there were countless fluctuations and the loosening of defences was fortunately very gradual, it was only after the increase in the number of sessions, which took place at the beginning of the second year, that breaks in treatment began to prove difficult and to confront us with nightmarish objects, the quintessence of a present persecutor replacing the absent object (Bion, 1962). It was during the second summer break, four terms after the beginning of treatment, that David wrote a poem about a father who is the source of all his misfortunes: a very fierce counterpart of the gullible father of the Richmond dream. He gave me the poem for his folder on the first session after the holiday break:

I never knew my gentle father
But if I look in the water, I see his face
Run till you reach the light of day
Because he is coming with love
He is coming with knives
A million fingers penetrating the dark
Lasers point from all
Lasers shining silently
Man is coming with knives
He'll take away your love and your life
Take him away.
Let me with woman stay.

With this poem I did not feel, in the countertransference, that I was only being confronted with a teenager's genital longings and anxieties, but with much more primitive feelings.

When the paternal function was perceived as the 'cruel cut' into our relationship (Father was there not to provide the link with Mother but to cut the link with Mother), what was revived in the transference were the grievances against the maternal grandmother who, David was told, had forced Mother to separate from him when he was still a baby; and against the father who left Mother totally unsupported and therefore contributed to the separation. Very significantly David dreamt, at this time, of the surgeon who had amputated his foot. He looked very much like a psychiatrist, about my age, whom David had repeatedly met in the Adolescent Department; David had a phantasy about this psychiatrist being my husband.

It is understandable that David should have taken such massive refuge in projective identification, as the notion of helpful parents seemed to be so lacking in his internal world. The paternal figure was so inimical and the maternal figure was so weak. I am sure that his needs to seduce me, entertain me, dazzle me were, at least partly, features of manic reparation: they were meant to engender life and excitement in the maternal object. Here I remember a song David wrote for a teenage girlfriend which he brought to one of his sessions: 'I'll make you laugh, I'll make you cry, I'll make your time fly by'; I think the song was also addressed to a depleted internal object. For at a very early infantile level, David had to prove to me that he would not be too heavy and too sad a child to carry. Before he started treatment he had written a poem that put across very poignantly his picture of a mother who cannot tolerate the sight of the child in pain:

Say goodbye, there don't cry
You'll only make her want to die
Go to sleep and lay heavily *on your own* heart. [my italics]

When I read this poem, I had the most vivid image of David as a small boy, saying goodbye to Mother without crying when she left the children's home after her visits, holding on with his eyes to the apricot or peach coloured coat.

David told me he remembered Mother visiting him at the children's home; he was wearing callipers and Mother said, 'I cannot pick you up, you are too heavy'. He also spoke about a friend of his, Robert, who was disabled too and always very depressed: 'Robert is so heavy, he would break anybody'. Then he dreamt that he was talking with me: he was telling me about two verses by Kahlil Gibran that had very much impressed him: 'The deeper pain carves into your being, the more joy it can contain'. But a friend of his, Mark, a disc jockey who was always very high, had appeared in the dream and interrupted him, saying, 'Stop talking heavy!'

So the mother in his mind could only cope with her disabled child if his stumps were hidden inside her cardigan. Indeed I have seen many photos of David's paintings and they contain a recurrent picture of the profile of a woman who is turning away. The mother who does not want to see or will only look if she can see her 'wonder boy' was the counterpart of the father of the cruel cut. Thus David told me at the beginning of his treatment that he was very little when he learned to ride his bike *without stabilisers*; a graphic image, perhaps, of his attempt to ride the course of life without the help of parents. When I became more acquainted with the texture of David's internal world, with the characters that inhabited his internal landscape, it became all the more understandable why he had to develop such massive defences against feelings of dependency.

The process of relinquishment of projective identification was long and painful both for David and for myself. Totally forgotten memories of the years in the children's home began to emerge, accompanied by tremendous bitterness and resentment; not only towards the father of the cruel cut, and the grandmother who had wanted him away, but the mother who might never have wanted him to be born. At times he felt very bitter about me and about what he called my 'Greenwich mean time', my sticking to schedule, my meanness. He felt excluded, especially at the weekends when he imagined me in the company of my psychiatrist husband and intact children. He was attending on Monday, Wednesday and Thursday and brought to one of his Monday sessions a poem he had written at the weekend. Its first lines read: 'Will you miss me, when the children say I love you, in the afternoon?'; this was in fact a very mild poem.

A rather witch-like figure appeared on more than one occasion in his dreams: it was the sister in charge of the ward where he had been hospitalised so many times as a child and where his foot was amputated when he was twelve years old. Her first name was Jane and he himself remarked on the considerable similarity to my first name. In one of the dreams Sister Lambert (he called her by her surname) had excluded him from a reunion of ex-patients that took place at the hospital because it was only meant for thalidomide children. In fact the origin of David's disability was unknown; he was not a thalidomide child. He had not even been entitled to the compensation reserved for this more 'fortunate' category, and his feelings of bitterness and resentment were overwhelming. They were much more prominent than feelings of sadness and for a time they completely dominated the transference relationship. David had never cried in his sessions and he told me very proudly that he did not remember the last time he had cried. However, a dream helped him remember. The dream was about a cat, Fluffy, which he used to be very fond of as a child, and in the dream Fluffy had come back to life. That was all he remembered, only a small fragment. But he could remember that the last time he had cried was when Fluffy was killed. He was then thirteen years old; the cat had run out into the road and it had been hit by a car. Fluffy had been damaged, but not killed. However, a passer-by had picked Fluffy up from the road and bashed him against the wall 'to put him out of his misery'. David still remembered that the man had used these very words to justify himself. He himself was sure that Fluffy would have survived had he been able to take him to the vet; 'Perhaps', he said, 'he might just have been a little lame'. In this same session he told me that his mother would certainly have had an abortion had she known about his disability before his birth; he was lucky, after all, not to have been 'put out of his misery', because he had both heard and read that many disabled children die 'accidentally' immediately after birth. The word 'accidentally' was pronounced with great sarcasm.

An external event precipitated a strong conflict between suspicion and an incipient trust in me. David had a conversation with a patient from the Adult Department whom he had repeatedly met in the lift. The man had been offered a time-limited period of therapy (30 sessions) and was approaching the end of his treatment. He suggested to David that he should ask me about the deadline I had in mind, because he was sure the offer of therapy was time-limited; that was the way we worked in the building. For David this was tantamount to being told that his relationship with me would be abruptly terminated, aborted. In the Wednesday session, when he told me about this encounter, which had taken place on the Monday, David was very agitated. He had slept very badly for two nights and nearly phoned me to find out if what he heard was true. He could not really believe it. Although he was still open to the whisperings of an internal and of an external saboteur, I felt that it was important that he had started questioning the truth of the matter before coming to his session; this pointed to a change in the quality of his internal object. Perhaps I was not so utterly unreliable, not so untrustworthy. Perhaps he was not under threat of sudden termination, of abandonment, of sliding away from Mother's lap, of not being able to hold on to her. You may remember that in the recurrent dream David had told me about, almost in passing, in the initial sessions, there was no indication that *Mother* was holding *him*.

I would now like to refer to a dream which does seem to point to a change in the nature of David's internal object, to an improvement in its capacity to hold him and to contain him. The dream was intimately related to the 'act of confidence' implicit in letting go of the grip of his eyes on me, for shortly after telling me about it, he suggested that he could attempt to use the couch. This was a change in the setting I had suggested when he started attending three times a week one year earlier, and many times after that.

> David dreamt that the house where he used to live with Mother as a small child was for sale. He was visiting it and it looked overwhelmingly beautiful, like a stately home (not like the real one, he said). David knew that he would never be able to buy it. A very rich man was going to buy the house. It was in need of repair and the man was going to take care of it. David went out in the garden, which also looked extremely beautiful, and he saw his mother. He started crying. Mother very tenderly put an arm around his shoulders and he put his head on her shoulder.

David was very close to tears in the session when he told me about this dream. He also seemed sure that he was crying in the dream, because he himself would have wished to be the rich man who could buy the house. It is true, I think, that the dream is about the pain of relinquishment of omnipotence and control of the object. The dream also seems to point to a relinquishment of manic reparation, for it is the paternal figure, the 'rich man', who has the means to restore the beautiful house/mother. It is only by coming out into the garden, by abandoning the projective identification that was so central to the 'dream of the Richmond house' that David could find the comforting mother who holds an arm around his shoulders. I felt very much in touch with him during this session and could very poignantly perceive his pain about the relinquishment, but also his relief. I remembered how strongly I had felt in the past that I could offer no real containment to David during the period when he was the magic 'fairy story boy'.

Shortly after this session David started using the couch. He could let go of the grip of his eyes on me as an external object only after he had begun to internalise an object capable of holding *him*. I shall make a brief reference to David's first session on the couch, which took place about two years after he started treatment. He told me that he had thought he was only going to have one pillow on the couch and had tried to get used to it by sleeping with only one pillow at home. He explained that he had been used for years to sleeping with two pillows, one next to the other; he liked rolling his head from one to the other. I had a very poignant picture, when he said that, of an infant safely held on Mother's lap, moving his head from one breast to the other; I also thought of the two pillows as a safeguard against falling, which was David's deepest anxiety. Perhaps there was, as the dream I have just described would suggest, the beginning of some trust in an internal object that made him feel he was being held. In the same session David told me that he had had a row, 'well a discussion', in the drawing class on the previous day. It concerned drawing from a model or drawing from one's mind, and David became very heated. He told Nicholas, the boy who preferred not to use external models, that if one draws from one's mind, 'one ends up with lots of stereotypes'; David preferred to have a model.

On his way home from college he realised that it was an interesting discussion to have on the day before he started using the couch, the day before he let go of me with his eyes. He himself suggested, and it seemed a very convincing interpretation, that it might have been like a discussion between two parts of himself. It seemed to point to a conflict between the part of David that was now able to 'let go', and a part full of trepidation about the ghost of old persecutory recurrent images: 'the men with knives', the profile of the woman with her head turned away; 'stereotypes', as David called them, that had also appeared in his dreams, in his poems, in his paintings. But needless to say, persecutory anxieties were indeed to return many times again, nor was the flight into projective identification a thing of the past. The months and years that followed did not represent a linear development and there were countless setbacks and very difficult patches.

I have chosen to illustrate this fragment of a long treatment in order to describe the process that led, through the repeated containment of persecutory anxieties, to the *beginning* of the internalisation of a benevolent and trustworthy object. The difficulty in letting go of the external object was obviously heightened in David because of his particular predicament. Indeed, his difficulty in relinquishing a visual hold is understandable when we think that from his birth, this was probably the only avenue *always* open to him for taking hold of an external object. It is also significant that he should have such a vivid early memory of a *visual* image: the apricot-peach colour of his mother's coat. David's love of painting, his sensitivity to beauty (so many beautiful houses in his dreams) again tell us of the importance of visual images and visual experiences.

In this chapter we have observed, in somewhat slow motion, a process which is atypical, but only in some respects. David's need to establish the initial internalisation of a containing object, before he could let go of an external one, is after all, not atypical. There is abundant evidence that such a sequence is necessary in development, both in our observational and clinical experiences. A child who is beginning to walk will only let go with one hand after he has taken a grip on a reliable object with the other. I think we can observe a similar process in terms of the transition from external to internal objects. The possibility of letting go of an external object, without experiencing excessive anxiety or developing crippling defences, is subsequent to the internalisation, or at least the *beginning* of the internalisation, of a reliable internal object.

7

Poor Feeders

I will begin to address the issue of rejection of dependent relationships in the context of 'infant observation'. This particular approach to the study of child development was introduced into the curriculum of the Child Psychotherapy Course at the Tavistock Clinic in 1948 by Esther Bick (Bick, 1964). I will give brief information about the methodology of infant observation and then quote some examples drawn from actual observations. My focus is on the observation of a 'poor feeder', for reasons which I will explain below.

Students observe a baby from birth to two years of age once a week for one hour on the same day of the week. Parents must not be previously known to them. Initial contact takes place with both parents before the birth of the baby, when the observer asks the parents for the favour of observing the development of their child as part of his or her current studies. Beyond the initial meeting, the observer's non-intrusive role generally becomes increasingly clear to the parents during the observation. Parents' expectations about having an expert on their premises providing advice, or parents' anxieties about being judged in their role, can, it is hoped, be gradually counteracted or dispelled by the observer's attitude and behaviour. Very often the attentive and regular presence of an observer enhances the parental interest in the details of their child's development. Observers are often struck by the improvement in the parents' observational skills when they hear about events which took place between observations, though some parents will pay greater attention to what their baby does, some to what the baby feels.

I was uncertain when confronted with the task of chosing the type of infant I would focus on in this chapter, but the first baby that came to my mind was a helpful infant called Jeremy who from the start valued his relationship to his mother and to her breast. The environment was not, at first, very supportive. Mrs Jones, Jeremy's mother, had very little hope of being able to establish breast-feeding with Jeremy. She had failed with her first child and initially made only a very half-hearted attempt with him. However, Jeremy's eagerness and whole-heartedness helped in setting in motion a benign circle. Mrs Jones did not hold her breast while feeding, so from very early on Jeremy was left to find his way to the nipple; he did so with great determination. He looked into his mother's eyes during the feed, often interrupting sucking to give her a beaming smile with a white mouth full of milk, only to make a beeline for the nipple again. On the other hand, I do not wish to describe the interaction of this nursing couple in too-glowing terms, or Jeremy as a 'perfect baby', immune from mixed feelings or anxiety. It was by no means the case. However, in spite of fluctuations and setbacks, what *could* be observed was an interaction where a 'good feeder' enabled his mother to give him probably the best she was capable of, and to acquire greater confidence about the value and the quality of what she had to give, at all levels. As members of the helping professions, we have all been confronted, at some point in our career, with the refreshing experience of feeling that what we had to offer was valued and appreciated; this generally enhances the capacity to perform at one's best.

It would have been easy to choose a series of examples starting with Jeremy, the good feeder, and go on to instances of patients craving for insight and students thirsty for knowledge, for both of whom Jeremy would have been the metaphor; but I wondered how helpful such an exercise would be. It may in fact be more valuable to reflect on the difficulties one encounters in doing our best work when faced with denigration or rejection. I decided therefore, as I have mentioned, to concentrate on the observation of a 'poor feeder' and reflect on the impact that his attitude had on his mother. This train of thought led me to choose the observation of a baby called Robert. I have selected only sequences related to feeding during Robert's first year because feeding appeared to be, from the day of Robert's birth, a very fraught and crucial issue. As the observations often took place when the father was at work, readers will note that Robert's father is almost never mentioned in these excerpts.

Robert

In the initial visit, prior to Robert's birth, Mrs Smith, the mother, had already told the observer that the baby would be bottle-fed. No reasons were given for the decision not to breast-feed, nor did the observer enquire, as this would have been far too intrusive a question. When we discussed the first meeting in a seminar, we felt that Mrs Smith was considerably lacking confidence in herself. I remember thinking to myself: 'Let's hope that she will give birth to a helpful baby (a Jeremy type of baby)'. Unfortunately, this was not the case.

I will now make use of the observer's (LG) notes.

The father telephoned LG on the day of Robert's birth, and invited him to visit in hospital. She saw Robert when he was 13 hours old, and wrote:

> Robert was in a bassinet next to mother's bed. She said that he'd had nothing from birth at 2.00am until 9.00am when he was given a little water which he didn't want. Then at 2.00pm mother was given a bottle for him, but Robert 'didn't know what to do with the teat, it must take some getting used to' (Mother's words). A nurse fed him from the bottle, but he threw most of it up. 'Still', mother said, 'he has found his thumb and has been sucking on it so he *must* be hungry'.

We were to learn later that Robert was virtually born with his thumb in his mouth; Mrs Smith asked the observer to come again in a couple of days in the hope of seeing him awake. I shall quote from the second observation. Robert is now two days old.

> At first he slept and made little stretching movements and his forehead was creased in a deep frown, a deep cleft on the lower lip was pulled up towards his mouth *as though he was sucking in the flesh*. Then he started to cry hard, one cry on each breath, followed by little shuddering inspirations. His tongue was a little crescent raised inside his mouth.

I go now to the third observation, when Robert is one week old and still in hospital:

> Mother told me she had great difficulty in getting him to bottle-feed and a paediatrician was called in and advised that Robert be taken to special care and put in a warm room. Mother said it was boiling in there and she cried when she saw the tube down his nose and taped to his cheek. She was told that he had repeatedly succeeded in removing the tube from his nose. She was also told that tube feeding was the only way to get him to keep his food down and that she should try feeding him again at intervals.

We could already hear that Mrs Smith feels rather at a loss when she says, 'Robert didn't know what to do with the teat', and we can see her tendency to abdicate in handing him over to the nurse. The three days when her baby had to be tube-fed drained her limited pool of hopefulness considerably. Mrs Smith went home on a Friday, and Robert stayed in hospital for ten more days. His mother went in as often as she could, to try to give him his bottle, but this was not at every feed. Although Robert left hospital when bottle-feeding was sufficiently established for him to be considered 'out of danger', the observer learned, on her first home visit, that the previous night 'he took two hours to take in one bottle and when father came home, he started crying and cried all evening. Father said he didn't know why he had bothered to come home'.

I will now quote from a visit when Robert is ten weeks old.

> Mother went back to cleaning the bathroom and I watched Robert asleep on his side, making a few sucking movements with his mouth, stopping, sucking a bit, stopping, his tongue was resting between his lips, so that he was actually *sucking his tongue*.

Here we can observe the persistence of patterns we were already seeing in the second observation: Robert seems to find comfort by sucking the inside of his mouth, sucking his tongue and turning to his thumb. Thumb-sucking looms large in the twentieth observation, when Robert is five months old:

> On his mother's lap, Robert sucked his thumb a great deal. He was then put in his canvas chair. Each time I gave him a soft toy he grabbed it, drew it to his mouth and put the thumb of his other hand into his mouth as well.

The transition to solids when Robert is six months old is fraught with difficulties. Robert is now putting more than one finger into his mouth:

> When Mother put him in his canvas chair, he moved about and protested before the first mouthful. The striking thing was that, after each mouthful, he put *three* fingers of his left hand deep into his mouth. Mother said twice during the feed: 'I wish I knew why these fingers have to go in'. The following week, while feeding, mother holds Robert's left hand with hers, so that he cannot put it into his mouth, but at every third mouthful or so he puts his right thumb into his mouth. Mother says, 'It wouldn't be so bad if it wasn't all his fingers, it would be all right if it were just his thumb'.

We can hear in this last remark and in the previous one – 'I wish I knew why these fingers have to go in' – an indication that Robert's mother feels that she is confronted with a worrying escalation. Most babies suck their thumbs, but she finds it hard to bear that Robert sucks three of his fingers and later the whole hand. She is disheartened and distressed, and she is particularly disconcerted when Robert's pattern of feeding changes dramatically and he starts bringing his cup to his mouth. To illustrate this I will quote from an observation when Robert is ten moths old:

> He seized his drinking cup and plunged it into his mouth, drinking with big gulps and a lot of noise. Mother pulled the cup down, Robert still hanging on to it so that he could take a breather, and the instant she let go, he whipped it into his mouth again. Big gulping and grasping noises. This pattern was repeated in quick motion until Robert had finished the drink and thrown the cup on the floor. Mother said: 'He always throws the cup away as soon as it is finished'.

I was greatly helped to understand the feelings of Robert's mother by my countertransference experience during the treatment of an anorexic patient who had been a very poor feeder in infancy, and steadily refused 'food for thought' in the early stages of her analysis with me. I learned that she had been persistently 'sucking the inside of her mouth' (her lower lip) from her early years and that she 'made it sore until it bled'. She also told me that she had been a tenacious thumb-sucker. The transference relationship acquainted me with her need to fall back on her own resources to avoid a dependent relationship in the same way as Robert, who turned to his five fingers. Interestingly, she improved a great deal after she was able to tell me about the secret biting and implicitly ask for my help in giving it a meaning. As it was, I could not see the biting inside her mouth, but had repeatedly interpreted the biting quality of her words.

An observation made when Robert was eleven months old confronts us with a literally 'breathtaking' sequence:

> Robert finished his food and came to his drink and what followed was dramatic. He seized the cup and took about four tasty, noisy swallows. Mother pulled the cup out of his mouth down on to the tray, Robert still holding on, he cried out loudly with frustration and anger. I do not remember hearing such a determined outraged sound from him before. He jammed the cup out of his mouth down on to the tray, Robert still holding on, he led out loud, breathless, angry cries, four even more desperate swallows and the drink was finished, Robert breathing fast and very frustrated. Then he gave a little cough and there was a heart-stopping moment when he could not breathe. His drink poured out of his mouth on to his bib, he gave one more cough and out poured the other half of the drink. Mother lifted him out of the high chair and set him on the floor, saying, 'Naughty Robert, you are a bad boy, you did that on purpose. My goodness, you've got a temper'.

Robert's mother clearly experiences her child's behaviour, at this point, as an act of defiance. He is obviously in distress but his mother is too distressed herself to empathise with his predicament and to attempt to find a meaning for it. I see this sequence as the example of a failure in the container function described by Bion (1962). If the mother (container) is unable to empathise with sensations and emotions which are meaningless and overwhelming for the baby, if she cannot perform the function of metabolising projections and rendering them meaningful in her mind, they remain unprocessed and indigestible for the child and return to him as 'nameless dread'. This process is graphically portrayed in the observation of Robert's bodily process of expulsion, for the 'heart-stopping moment' described by the observer could be seen as an experience of nameless dread (Bion, 1962).

We see how a very complicated pattern *related to both nature and nurture* evolves in the relationship of this problematic nursing couple. In the following observation, we see the mother remaining at a distance while Robert is crying, as if she has given up hope that she could be of any help to her disconcerting child:

> Robert finished his food and mother put the drinking cup in front of him; he waited a moment, then picked it up eagerly and took a mouthful and immediately started to cough. Tears sprang out of his eyes, a mouthful of liquid poured out on to his bib and he cried bitterly putting the cup back on the tray and looking at it. Mother sat watching him without making a move, then Robert picked up the cup and tried again and exactly the same thing happened. Coughing prevented him from swallowing, he lost a mouthful of liquid, cried bitterly and angrily, put down the cup, this time leaving it sitting in front of him. Mother *remained unmoving although tears were pouring down Robert's cheeks*, and she said to me, 'You can see he just refuses liquids'.

As the observation suggests, Robert's mother found it increasingly difficult to sustain confidence in her capacity to give her child something that he might accept and appreciate more than his own thumb or five fingers. Her attempts in reaching out to him became fainter and fainter. It was naturally very painful for the observer to witness the deterioration of the relationship in the nursing couple. Fortunately, on more than one occasion, this mother could communicate her distress to her, and, as I have seen in many observations, sympathetic listening provided containment for some of her anxiety. However, the observer was never asked for advice, neither do I think that an advisory role would be compatible with an observation (Bick, 1964).

Applications

I would now like to move to the work setting and see how one can apply within it the insights gained in the observational setting. In fact Robert's difficulties came very vividly to mind in the course for teachers at the Tavistock Clinic, when a primary school teacher presented his problems with a boy called Paul.

Paul

Nine-year-old Paul was described by his teacher Mr Duncan as an 'unteachable clever child'. When the teacher attempted to help him assimilate some basic concepts of mathematics, he would say that he could not be bothered with maths because his subject was space technology, or would complain that the teaching was 'not up to his own standard'. Mr Duncan felt at a loss with him, and I was reminded of Robert's mother's comment, 'You can see he just refuses liquids'. Paul was also the only child in the class who treated a girl with learning difficulties, Mary, with ruthless contempt; for instance, he drew a picture of Mary with her head down the lavatory.

At a parents' meeting, the teacher learned that Paul's mother was a disheartened woman who wished 'her little boy gave her a chance to help him'; she had heard Paul cry at night more than once, but she knew from previous experience that had she gone to him he would certainly have pushed her away and denied that he had ever been crying. She knew that Paul needed a helping hand and was very miserable, but she felt that her hands were completely tied; like Robert's mother she was at a loss as to how to help him. She was also concerned about his learning difficulties, and she said she thought he must have a good mind because he was quite an expert about anything to do with outer space.

Mr Duncan told us that at that meeting, Paul's mother had helped him to understand the feeling that this boy evoked in him. He could sense, although he had never seen him crying, that he was a very unhappy child, continually trying to deny his weakness and refuse any dependency. After this communication there was also a considerable shift in the mood of the teachers' group. At first they had reacted with profound distaste to the description of Paul's drawing of Mary. I suggested that, unsavoury as that piece of behaviour might be, we could try and understand it in terms of Paul's need to disown and locate in someone else a 'substandard' part of himself for which Mary became a very suitable receptacle (after all, he himself was not achieving in school).

His drawing showed how he wished to flush down the drain this denigrated, unacceptable aspect of himself, so that he could preserve an unblemished, self-idealised picture of Paul 'the space technologist'.

As we were discussing the substandard part of Paul, Mr Duncan reminded us that he had been told in no uncertain terms that *his* teaching methods were 'substandard'. Did Paul perhaps wish for him to feel a little handicapped as well? The group laughed at this comment, but I wondered whether we might not be trying to see a *comic* aspect in Paul's behaviour, because we all found it hard to stay with its *tragic* quality. He was a boy obviously in need of teaching and nurturing, most of all of being understood; he was, however, so intolerant of any feeling of dependency that he tried to ignore and disown it, attempting instead to foster 'better teaching standards' in his teacher. Yet he was alone with his tears. His mother was not to know what the tears were about, nor were we. We could only guess. Perhaps Paul's system of defences might not after all be so water-tight (tear-proof); perhaps the under-achiever in himself represented by Mary did not go down the drain. Perhaps feelings of inadequacy and loneliness confronted him when he was alone at night.

Paul's mother was probably right in feeling that she would be perceived as trespassing had she gone into Paul's bedroom while he was crying, and we then discussed what could be most helpful in terms of Mr Duncan's relationship with Paul: it was not a matter of breaking and entering into possible chinks in the boy's armour, for instance at times when Paul looked pathetic. Mr Duncan agreed he did not wish to take Paul off-guard and confront him with his weakness when 'he looked wobbly'. He could, on the other hand, resist the temptation to bend over backwards and find ways to coax Paul into accepting some of the 'food for thought' he was offering, as he felt he had done in the past. That could be seen as the equivalent of the manoeuvring some mothers of poor feeders do in order to entice their children into eating. Such behaviour is often the consequence of feeling so disheartened by the continual refusal of what is being offered that teachers and mothers alike may be overwhelmed by the unbearable pain of rejection, and, somehow, see no alternative to playing tricks or, as one of the teachers in the group put it: 'Devising the right commercial in order to sell a poor product'. Mr Duncan told us that when he had felt at the end of his tether or at a loss with Paul, he had actually, more than once, begun to doubt the quality of his teaching. As we saw, Paul had a strong need to lodge his feelings of inadequacy in someone else, and his disowning of such feelings through projection was probably very powerful. As

Melanie Klein wrote: 'The object into whom badness (the bad self) is
projected becomes the persecutor *par excellence* because it has been
endowed with all the bad qualities of the subject' (Klein, 1952, p.69).
Mr Duncan had said very sensitively that it would be a matter of
'finding the right sort of smile' when Paul confronted him again with
some contemptuous assessment of his performance as a teacher: not a
sarcastic smile but a smile conveying the feeling that while he understood how Paul felt, he was not subscribing to his poor assessment of
school and teachers. Should this experience even slightly decrease Paul's
self-idealisation, it could help him descend from outer space (his interest in space technology was certainly not accidental), and might
eventually enable him to accept a helping hand. There seemed to be a
hope that, given time and a *number* of experiences where there was no
collusion with Paul's pattern of defences, he could gradually develop
trust in somebody capable of understanding and 'feeding him' without
making him utterly dependent. In fact, the group was left wondering
about this because Paul had only one more year in primary school
(though fortunately Mr Duncan was going 'to go up' with him into the
last year), and the transition to secondary school was very likely to
present further problems. However, we did hear about Paul three times
during the course of the year and we had reason to gather some hope.

Marco

I would like to enlarge on the theme of splitting and projection
exemplified by Paul's attitude towards Mary, that is, the process of
disowning parts of oneself and lodging them in someone else. I will use
for this purpose a series of much shorter examples, and the first one is
drawn from the observation of a ten-month-old boy called Marco
whose relationship with his parents had been very close. We are looking
at an interesting development which occurred when the parents decide
that Marco should enter a creche. Despite reciprocal tenderness in his
relationship with both parents, one week after entering the creche
Marco is trying to become a 'tough boy' and to conform to a culture
where it was felt that 'children shouldn't cry'. I quote from the notes of
an observation which took place one week after Marco had entered the
creche:

> Elena is on the carpet – tears running down her cheeks. Marco, who had
> been playing until then, throws his toy away and quickly grabs the little
> girl by the hair. I am near him and try to hold him back and say, 'You are

hurting the little girl, but every time I let go of his hand, Marco grabs Elena's hair hard. The little girl cries even more desperately and Marco stares at her very seriously, obviously ready to repeat the action. Holding his hand, I guide him towards another corner of the room, but just as he arrives there, a baby of six months who all this time had been quiet, begins to cry and immediately Marco goes over to him and starts to pull his hair. The nursery teacher stops him and tells him that it is not nice, but Marco looks at her with a serious expression and repeats the gesture. The teacher says, 'They are all like that, the moment a child is crying the others are ready to hit him' and she takes the smaller baby into her arms to protect him.

In a later observation Marco is described as less 'well adapted'; now he is crying himself and we can see how he is strongly encouraged to become tough again:

> The teacher tells mother, 'yesterday Marco stopped crying almost imme-diately', and then turning to him, 'Come, come, you see you are making Mummy feel bad', and she takes him in her arms and tries to take off his sweater, but he bends himself backwards leaning towards the floor instead of against her shoulder. Mother looks on in silence; she is very pale. One can feel she is suffering. The teacher says to her, 'It is better for you to leave now, I will take the child in and you will see he will calm down right away'. The mother replies, 'Why can't he be like that child there? That one never cries', and points to a child of six or seven months playing on the floor.

The observation of Marco lends itself to fruitful reflections in terms of group dynamics and adaptation to group culture, in particular the acquisition of a tough attitude as a defence against the pain of separa-tion. Fortunately this trend was not firmly entrenched and, during the second year of observation, the observer and the seminar group saw him gradually acquiring enough strength to tolerate his vulnerability.

Reactions to Separation

To continue on the theme of splitting and projecting one's vulnerable aspects, I will now move to the description of children in a children's home who have been told by their worker Julie that she would be leaving in about a month's time; she had been there for four years. The quotations are from Julie's notes:

> Roger sat wagging his finger at me: 'You're not leaving – I'm not going to allow you to leave, who am I going to fight with?' He then wondered

who would do my work and who would be on duty when I should be. Stephen shouted out, 'I'll take Julie's place'. Charlie was sitting silent, his eyes were beginning to fill with tears. Kevin entered the room – I told him. There was a momentary look of dismay, then, 'Hey, Jimmy we're going to have a booze-up'. Shortly afterwards he and Robert were in the TV room: Roger said, 'Hey, Kevin, have you heard, Julie's leaving, isn't it a shame?' Kevin grunted, engrossed in TV. Charlie came up and put his arms around me – 'You're not leaving me, are you?' and held me for a while. Sandra looked at me. 'Are you?' 'Yes.' She hugged me as if to console me: 'Never mind', she said.

Margaret came home from school, I said I was glad she had come back as I wanted to tell her something. Margaret sat at the table, cut a slice of bread and piled it up with jam – she spoke with her mouth full – 'Pity, I'll have no one to talk to', and she cut another slice of bread. She continued eating non-stop for about half an hour. That evening Roger put on some loud pop music and most children danced frantically, taking no notice of me. Charlie came close to me and said loudly so that I could hear him in spite of the music, 'You are not going to leave me, are you Julie, I don't want you to go, why can't you stay?' I could see that he had been crying. Charlie said, 'I know, I'll get you a present. I'll buy you a record'. On his third visit to the kitchen he asked me again, 'Why do you have to leave here?' I explained. 'I know, I'll get you a present, not a record though, what would you like?' 'Something that reminds me of you.' 'How about a photo? I have one upstairs', and he bounded off.

Later that evening Charlie had fallen asleep on the settee. At a quarter past nine he awoke. I went over to him and gently suggested that he go to bed. He turned his head against the back of the settee and began to cry. When he quietened down, I took him up to bed.

Charlie shares his room with Kevin, Peter and Stephen. During the night I heard shouts coming from that room. When I arrived Kevin was hitting Charlie fiercely on his head with a pillow. As I entered the room, he stopped and said, 'You see if you can shut him up, he keeps sobbing and we want to go to sleep'.

We can see here how the crying child is not tolerated by the tough culture of the children's home. Charlie, who shows his distress, is upsetting the system, just as crying children upset the system in Marco's nursery. Tears have to be silenced with loud pop music or pushed down the throat by eating vast amounts of food, as Margaret did. The crying child reminds the others of the weaker and more vulnerable and tender part of themselves that they wish to forget about. Marco's hair-pulling in the nursery gives us a glimpse of the type of reaction we can expect to see in much older children, as in the sequence I have just given from Julie's notes.

Discussion

In this chapter, I am relying on the hypothesis that a psychoanalytic frame of reference can be used to understand interaction, or lack of interaction, in a variety of contexts. It must be apparent that the examples I selected share some features, but it may be useful to highlight the nature of the links I saw between Robert the baby and Paul the schoolboy, as well as the links between the toddler Marco within the group and the group dynamics emerging in the children's home.

In the first series of examples I saw the rejection of concrete or symbolic nourishment as a common denominator. We saw that Robert often blocked access to his mouth with his thumb and literally refused *concrete* nourishment. Something similar was expressed by Paul in a more symbolic form as he manifested, in his learning difficulties, a rejection of the 'food for thought' that his teacher was offering him. If one then compares, for instance, the observation of Robert with the observation of babies who *do* form an attachment to the source of nourishment (Jeremy, for instance) we see how they are repeatedly exposed to pain and frustration because of not being able to control when and how often the mother or the maternal substitute provides the breast or the bottle and gives of herself and of her attention. Babies who form such attachments often have to negotiate a very painful experience of loss at the time of weaning. For a long time Robert appeared to sustain for a long time a phantasy of controlling the source of his comfort; he protected himself from the painful feelings connected with dependency and the fear of loss first by using his thumb, and then escalating to three fingers or even to five fingers to fill his mouth. His fingers were *always* available.

Paul confronts us with a similar pattern: we could see his 'space technology', the subject that takes him into an outer space of his own, as somehow the equivalent of Robert's thumb. Paul initially fobs off his teacher's invitation to occasionally take his space technology off his mind, 'his thumb out of his mouth' in order to make space for different nourishment. We can also see how he engenders feelings of extreme helplessness, both in his teacher and in his mother, as Robert did. That is, Paul could not face his own helplessness, but he had a great capacity to engender feelings of helplessness in others. I think his teacher was helped by beginning to see that Robert's behaviour need not only be perceived as an attack. It was only after he disengaged himself from a potential battle of wits and began to perceive the miserable child hidden inside the 'space technologist' that he was able to make better contact with Paul.

I would like now to clarify the frame of reference I used in choosing the second series of examples. A similar mechanism to one operative in Paul appears to me to underlie the behaviour of the children ganging up on Charlie in the children's home. For Charlie lends himself very suitably to representing the softness and the fear of loss that the other children cannot afford to experience. When an unwanted aspect is lodged in someone else (at times a suitable receptacle for it), the receptacle can itself become quite intolerable. So I would suggest that a mechanism came into operation here whereby the vulnerable, soft, crying child had to be attacked and obliterated, '*made to shut up*', as the gang in the bedroom very clearly told Julie. What we can see in the toddler Marco is a less hardened version of this process. At one point he is attacking a crying child but then we see him shifting back to being a crying child himself. In fact, he had a supportive enough environment to be able to negotiate painful feelings, and in later observations showed that he did not remain a hardened child. Indeed, the observation of Marco appears to me helpful in looking at a process in slow motion, at a stage where it has not as yet become rigid. It is easy to guess the reasons why Marco might be pulling Elena's hair, when we know that he was *at that moment* himself struggling with a feeling of loss and quite possibly the wish to cry.

Throughout this chapter I have been relying on the general hypothesis that early infantile aspects continue to be present in later stages of normal development, and are particularly evident in pathological development. And one of the enrichments of the experience of infant observation is that it sharpens one's capacity to notice infantile aspects in children of all ages, *even when they are elusive*. In fact they might be a vital core in all individuals. We cannot see the roots of trees: but there is no live tree without roots.

8

Reversal of the
'Container/Contained' Relationship

I would like, first of all, to clarify what I mean by the reversal of the 'container/contained' relationship, and then talk about this theme using some clinical material. It is rare to meet the phenomenon 'in pure culture', so to speak, but it can happen that a child, at times a baby, still desperately in need of containment, is exposed to the experience of being used as a *receptacle* (this word is more appropriate than container) of massive projections. Often it is the very adult who should have provided the function of containment, had he or she been fit to do so, who projects into the child or the baby. I came across this problem mainly in cases where the parents of patients were psychotic or border-line.

I have been interested in this theme – of the child as a recipient of projection, or the reversal of the container/contained relationship – for a number of years. I began to formulate some hypotheses on this subject mainly since I worked, either in an assessment setting or in therapy, with eating disorder patients. The hypothesis I formulated helped me to reflect, somewhat with hindsight, on the case of a psychotic young girl who was twelve when I started seeing her.

Natasha

Natasha had been diagnosed as suffering from mental handicap when she was still very little. There was no evidence of organic causes. By the time I started treating her five times a week, following the advice of the psychiatrist who had assessed her, Natasha had spent all her primary school and a short period of so-called secondary school in two different residential institutions for mentally subnormal children. She had some-how confirmed the diagnosis of handicap by her functioning during the years of latency; the parents, who had both suffered traumatic experiences earlier in their lives, had never questioned the diagnosis. Natasha was beginning to show some signs of pubertal development (she was rather a big girl for her age), when she was transferred from the primary school to the secondary school at the age of eleven. She started to show some alarming symptoms and was referred to a child guidance clinic for assessment. Although it was extremely difficult to reconstruct her history, it seems that up to that time Natasha had held herself together with an obsessional carapace, a very rigid carapace. For instance, she had won a prize in the primary school for her ability in constructing a variety of objects using glue and match sticks, one such being a large doll's house. However, the 'glue' – the connective tissue – which precariously held Natasha's personality together did not hold against the impact both of pubertal development and the change of institutions. The fragments – 'the matchsticks' – started getting unstuck and a chink, an ever wider chink, in the obsessional carapace started opening.

An extremely persecutory delusional system gradually developed. Natasha was terrified that fleas could penetrate the orifices of her body, even the pores of her skin. It had become almost impossible to convince her to change her clothes and there was no way of getting her to change from her day clothes into her pyjamas when she went to bed. She also refused to take a bath. For some months she was only able to eat during her sessions; she refused for a time both to talk and to eat elsewhere. She was now drinking with a straw, keeping her lips shut very tight and muttering in a very indistinguishable way without opening her mouth. She continually repeated a sort of exorcising litany, full of 'keep away, keep away', which was addressed to the fleas that she saw everywhere. Natasha did actually have some visual hallucinations, but in spite of the serious problem about her personal hygiene, real fleas never appeared.

Between one litany and the next, I learned in a fragmentary way that the fleas could enter the orifices of her body or even the pores of her skin, if she got undressed. She often kept her fingers on her ears during the session, but she was frightened that something, even my words, could get into her nostrils. She then widened her hands – closing her nose between two fingers and using her thumb to close her right ear. Later she started to use a pillow which became very important in blocking access to one of her ears. When her nose was shut, she breathed by minimally opening her lips and, as I have said, the sounds which came out of her mouth were often quite difficult to decipher.

Retrospectively, I can probably better understand at least some of the contributory factors in Natasha's delusional system. At this point, it is worth mentioning that throughout Natasha's analysis, I was continuously in touch with the colleagues who were working separately with his parents, for when Natasha started her analysis, her parents were also offered help. Mother accepted more intensive help, father accepted a once-weekly session only. I now have reason to think that Natasha was exposed, when a very small child, to massive projections. Her mother was admitted to hospital for puerperal depression after her birth and her father, who looked after Natasha when mother was in hospital, as well as often after her return, suffered from more silent symptoms. Father had lost a good part of his family in the Nazi holocaust and was quite obsessed by the theme of war criminals. His phantasy about his possible role/function in the capture of war criminals had some delusional aspects. So my hypothesis today is that Natasha was the recipient of massive projections in a family where there were no other adults capable of offering containment, either to the infantile parts of her very distressed parents, nor to her. Natasha might have protected herself from this devastating experience by retreating into a state of pseudo-stupidity which was wrongly diagnosed as mental deficit. She held herself together with her obsessional armour during the years of latency (I know very little about her pre-latency years), and she became identified with the other residents of the special school she had been resident in, some of whom were very seriously handicapped. Sometimes, in a very disturbing way, she took on the appearance of a mental defective, offering a very realistic picture of one. However, the psychiatrist who saw Natasha when she was already in the secondary school and who decided that she should be removed from a school, for the mentally defective, was quite adamant that there was no evidence of mental handicap.

Natasha had developed some important relationships in the primary school, even though, or perhaps because, the environment colluded with her defences, her pseudo-stupidity. Nobody expected Natasha to function any better than she did and this limited her learning very much; she was considered very good at doing things with her hands, but not with her head. The loss of the first school must have been a traumatic experience for her in the sense of the original meaning of the word 'surgical trauma' (Laplanche and Pantalis, 1980, p.465), that is: a wound. It produced a laceration in the carapace of her defensive system. Having been uprooted from a known environment probably contributed to this at least as much as the onset of puberty.

The reason why I am talking about Natasha's breakdown, after so many years, is that I think that her delusional system offers an extremely graphic image of the same mental state which I have encountered in a more hidden or veiled form in less disturbed patients (whom I have either seen myself or heard about in supervision). You will remember, for example, the terror Natasha had of fleas entering the pores of her skin, the orifices of her body. She had difficulties in finding enough fingers on her hands to close all the orifices; she was terrified that something could enter into her nose if she shut her ears with her fingers; she had difficulty in finding a compromise in order to breathe, in order to eat. It is interesting that she perceived the excretory processes as a way of freeing himself from persecutors; they were not affected by her pathology. The rectum was perceived, however, as a possible avenue of access; therefore it is very striking that she was not frightened about sitting on the lavatory.

We know from our clinical experience how overwhelming the weight of psychotic projections in our countertransference is, and how we need the help of supervisors or colleagues in order to metabolise them. One can well imagine how impossible to digest they must be for a very small child. I am suggesting that the indigestible experience of being invaded by persecutory objects, which could originally have been projections, might constitute one (I would like to stress *one*) of the nuclei around which Natasha's delusional system was structured.

As I have said, Natasha needed to protect every possible access route to her body – her nostrils, her ears, her mouth, her eyes. She often kept them shut and even feared that the pores of her skin could be invaded, penetrated by fleas. This was the reason why she didn't get undressed and didn't take a bath. It was a distressing experience for me when for the first time during a session, Natasha took off a sock which was stuck to her foot as if she were taking off a piece of dead skin. In fact little by little the terror of being invaded diminished slightly so that Natasha, who felt gradually more contained, became less terrified and agreed more often to change her clothes. It was at this time that she gave me a very vivid experience of how violent the phantasy of intrusion into her skin was. Natasha managed to get hold of a tiny bit of skin on my hand and she pulled. She had long nails and she managed to lift a little skin, holding the edge of it as if she were going to skin me. She looked at me straight in the eyes with a very sadistic sneer, and said 'You are not crying – you must be God'. I pulled my hand away. There was minimal damage but I needed an enormous amount of help to metabolise the projections that had got into me. Natasha certainly used her eyes as an organ of projection, and perhaps something very terrifying had been projected into her by her psychotic mother with her eyes when she was a small child.

I am by no means undervaluing the importance of other phantasies which were conglomerated in the delusional system: the terror of being invaded by persecutory babies/fleas (Meltzer, 1979); the terror of a return of the minute fragments (Bion, 1957) that Natasha and her objects (Klein, 1946) were split into. The exorcising litany she always repeated seemed initially to represent some protection from total disintegration. I have been highlighting one particular component in Natasha's delusional system which originally might have been connected *with a terror of being invaded by projections.*

Leila

I shall now give a brief description of a European colleague's case where the reversal of the container and contained relationship appears to loom very large. The patient is at the moment of writing at the beginning of her second year of psychotherapy, which takes place on a three-times-weekly basis. Leila is eighteen years old and could remain in the institution where she lives until she is twenty-five. The therapist who is treating her was given very full information about her history before she started the treatment; she would have preferred information to come from the patient but she had to fit in with the method of work of the institution.

Leila was born in Tunisia, and is the eldest of four children. When she was twelve her parents left Tunis to visit an aunt in Granada in Spain saying that they were going to be away for a long weekend, for four days. They left Leila with her three brothers, the eldest of whom was nine at the time; there was a five year old and the third one was less than one year old. The parents had relatives in Granada and they were helped to find work and decided to stay there. About a week after they had left, Leila was informed that her parents were not going to come back and she was left to look after her three brothers. Apparently there was a total breakdown of communication with the family, and only a female cousin of the mother and the cousin's husband visited regularly. Leila herself said she was 'perfectly capable' of looking after her three brothers. (This is what she told one of the teachers in the school which she attended after she came to live in a children's home.) Following a sustained period of sexual abuse by the male maternal cousin already mentioned, she had a breakdown leading to a suicide attempt. Leila thought that the wife was not totally unaware of what was happening but she turned a blind eye, causing Leila to attempt to drown herself by jumping from a rock close to the beach into the sea. A guard threw himself into the sea and saved Leila, and the parents who lived in Granada were informed of the attempted suicide. They came to Tunis and initially planned to take all the children to Spain, but then left with only the three boys. Apparently, mother has a very white skin while father is very dark, and Leila is the only one of the siblings who has a dark skin. She is convinced that she was left behind in Tunisia because her mother is ashamed of the colour of her skin.

According to the history Leila gave to the teacher, she lived subsequently with 'relatives' (not the cousins). A few months later, she was sent a ticket to fly to Spain and join the family. When she arrived she realised that mother could not cope with the small children and that mother had asked her to join them because she needed help with child care. Initially, Leila fitted into this role, which she said 'she enjoys'. At present she is looking after the children of a Spanish family as an au pair, and she intends to become a nursery school teacher.

There seems to be some evidence that, having missed out on the experience of containment and mothering, Leila somehow entered the maternal role in a sort of self-idealisation whereby she could mother herself and other children, and all needy aspects were thus disowned, split off and projected into those she looked after. However, a serious breakdown occurred when Leila was taken to the Tunisian Embassy by her mother to sign some papers 'in order to obtain a permit of residence'. It turned out that Leila had signed a paper that ratified her marriage at the age of seventeen to a man who was at the time thirty-four years old and was probably mother's lover. Leila's father is a very passive man and the mother, according to Leila, then felt that she could keep her lover on the premises as he was by then the lawfully married husband of her daughter. Leila refused to have a sexual relationship with the man, and about two months after the marriage had taken place she took a serious overdose. She was taken to hospital in time to have her stomach washed out and was subsequently admitted to the residential institution where she still lives. She has now lost contact with her family of origin. She has developed fluency in Spanish but has completely forgotten Arabic, the only language she spoke when she was in Tunisia. She has also recently changed her name from Leila to Carmen.

I will refer to just some aspects of the relationship Leila established (and had considerable difficulties in establishing) with her psychotherapist. My focus will mainly be Leila's reaction to holiday breaks. The first break, which occurred at Christmas, was not acknowledged as a significant experience by Leila at all. During the break, an accident occurred: Leila fell, sliding on her back for the whole length of an elevator in a department store. She was badly bruised and some of her ribs were cracked. She was taken to hospital and soon recovered. It seems particularly significant that she fell down a long drop not having acknowledged in any way the experience of having been 'dropped' by her therapist when she left her for the very crucial Christmas holiday. Leila has converted to Catholicism and repudiated her allegiance to the Moslem religion, just as she had completely forgotten Arabic. It is striking that instead of thinking about the experience of being dropped she enacted it, falling down the elevator of the department store and damaging herself. The 'fall' is also very reminiscent of the suicide attempt when she threw herself into the sea in Tunisia. It is also significant in that case and in the case of the subsequent suicide attempts, that Leila somehow acted out her suicidal impulses in circumstances where she was likely to be rescued. Something 'on the side of life' appears to be present in this profoundly damaged girl.

The reaction to the subsequent holiday was much more manic. Leila became promiscuous and went out with a number of young men, having abandoned a man of whom she had been very fond at the time when she was cheated into getting married. She had decided to commit suicide and said 'she didn't want to hurt him'. The man she abandoned was in fact her godfather, a reliable and devoted young man. But the youngsters Leila mixed with and with whom she had some sexual contact (not full sexual relationships) during the therapist's Easter break were of a very different sort; it looked as if she could not bear a sexual relationship with someone other than a sort of 'abuser'.

The therapy has been characterised, from the start, by an extreme imperviousness in Leila's attitude. After about one year of treatment she has recounted part of her history to her therapist. What Leila said felt true in the countertransference – she didn't seem to put experiences across in a sensational way, and for a long time her talking was the exception, not the rule. Although she lived in the residential institution and the therapist provided her sessions there, she always arrived late to the session and spent at least 10 minutes in silence at the beginning of each session. Always dressed in black, she was for quite some time totally impervious to interpretation either about her looks or the nature of her silence. Her identification was not at this point with the 'all-giving mother' but with the 'impervious unavailable object', and it was the therapist who had to suffer the pain which was caused by that sort of object. A girl who has been grossly deprived of the experience of containment has been able to use the therapeutic relationship in order to project painful feelings: the therapist has felt cut off, helpless, quite unable to reach her. One can well imagine that those are feelings that Leila must have experienced in the depths when she was abandoned by her parents and, later, when she was betrayed by her mother in the arranged marriage. Her capacity to project and make the therapist feel her pain seem to be hopeful signs of her developing some confidence in an object that can take the pain she cannot bear – the pain of the child who is not taken notice of, who is cut off and rejected. However, this type of splitting and projection cannot continue to function when the therapist goes away on holiday, and this is when Leila gets in touch with the feeling of not being contained and acts out the very concrete experience of 'being dropped' by falling down the stairs of the elevator.

I am extremely impressed by the work Leila's therapist has been able to carry out with such an impervious patient. Some elements of trust are beginning to be established in their relationship: some dreams are beginning to emerge; Leila is not as silent and impenetrable as she used to be at the beginning. I myself have used this case as a striking example of projection into a young girl of feelings that were impossible for her to metabolise, that is, as an example of total reversal of the container/contained relationship. Leila has been at the receiving end of psychic pain it would have been hard to deal with without developing massive defences. One of these defences is projective identification with the 'all-giving mother'; another is the imperviousness to contact that her therapist has experienced.

The first type of projective identification has a pathological nature: identification with an idealised object who can give all and needs nothing. The second type of projective identification – the pain that Leila projects into her therapist – has a very different function, for this function is intimately related to the object she is projecting into. Leila is telling her therapist about the feeling of being pushed off, rejected, unwanted; she has, in this case, a container that can process these feelings and is gradually giving them back to her in a way that can be thought and spoken about. It becomes extremely difficult whenever holidays approach; however, reactions to holidays do appear to offer some sign of hope that Leila is, after all, capable of developing an attachment, albeit a very controlling one: she still cannot bear to perceive the separateness of an object who can come and go. But this process could eventually, if gradually, lead to an experience of real dependency.

Lastly, I would like to add that one of the symptoms Leila suffers from is a recurrent although not stable bulimia. It possibly represents a way of expressing her repressed wish to take in voraciously from an impervious object who is not prepared to give; at the same time she gets rid of what she has taken inside by vomiting. This is possibly perceived as persecutory because in phantasy she has demolished the impervious object in her bingeing.

Work in this case is still very much in process but I think it is possible, given the profound commitment of the therapist, that there might be a favourable outcome and that this girl, who has been at the receiving end of unbearable projections, might gradually develop the experience of accepting a container who can contain her.

Gillian

I would like now to talk briefly about another patient, a young mother whom I started seeing three times a week a few years ago. Gillian was twenty at the time, and her little boy, Sam, was four months old. I saw mother and baby together for some months, as Sam would otherwise have had to be left with his father, a heroin addict; Gillian was trying to disengage herself from this boyfriend. She had written to the Tavistock describing her predicament quite concisely, telling us that her father had left when she was ten years old, that her mother first developed an alcohol problem and now a psychiatric illness and was in a psychiatric hospital. I will quote from her words: 'I haven't got used to the idea of my father leaving and now I must get used to the idea of my mother leaving. I am only nineteen, I have just had a baby and I feel desperate'. Gillian did not tell us in the letter that she had a sister, Cecily, who was about one year younger than herself; neither did she say anything about her boyfriend or about his problems.

The sessions Gillian shared with Sam until a satisfactory baby sitting arrangement could be found were very difficult for her. Gillian could not bear me to turn my attention to Sam, and when Sam became in any way demanding, she gave him the breast and this kept him quiet, but not for very long. Sam also wanted the attention of Gillian and he wanted my attention too. If Gillian started talking with me and somehow forgot about him, Sam would get his head out of the very large jumper Gillian used to wear (she just lifted her jumper in order to feed Sam; she never uncovered her breast) and start whining. Often Sam put a hand in Gillian's mouth and made it impossible for her to go on talking. There was no question that, at this time, Gillian would also have liked to put her hand in my mouth and bring my attention back to her when sometimes, as was natural, I spoke to Sam.

The letter I referred to spoke of a number of losses, the recent loss of mother, the loss of father, but did not make any reference to another important loss. This took place when Gillian was only one year old and Cecily was born, and was, I think, quite a dramatic event in her life. Our session somehow reproduced a situation where Gillian had to share my attention with another child, just as she had to share mother's attention with Cecily. Sam could easily become a sibling instead of a son, and thus an ideal recipient for the projections of psychic pain related to a loss which Gillian could not tolerate herself.

This use of Sam as a receptacle of devastating projections, albeit not psychotic ones, took place during an interruption of about 10 days at Christmas, the first break in our work. When Gillian came back in January, I noticed that Sam, who was sitting in his pushchair and was not taken out of the pushchair by her, had a cold sore on his lower lip, and that he was very restless. Gillian told me almost immediately that she had started weaning him and that she had already 'got rid of two feeds' (incidentally, she had missed 5 sessions because of the break) but it was a fight. Sam did not want the bottle and he was spitting the milk. Not very long after this communication, Sam, who was still sitting in the pushchair during the session, brought up quite a large amount of milk (I wonder now if he was beginning to get rid of some projections).

Gillian looked after him in an absent-minded way, full of rage. She turned to me and said 'I could kill him'. I turned towards Sam and I told him 'It isn't true that Mummy wants to kill you, she wants to get rid of a little Gillian who is very angry with me because I disappeared for 10 days'. I very much doubt that Sam could have understood this interpretation word for word, but he must have felt somehow reassured because he gave me a very sad smile. I felt he was telling me 'and I am the one who has paid for it'. I interpreted to Gillian what I thought Sam was trying to tell me; she did not accept this reintegration of her infantile part with good grace. And in this session I would learn that Gillian had spent quite a lot of time with Charlie, the boyfriend from whom she tried to separate during November. Charlie had given Gillian 'a lot of dope' as a Christmas present (this was said in a very provocative way). Projections were therefore beginning to fall in to the right receptacle, or better, the right container, for I felt taken over by a strong feeling of anxiety; anxiety which had the colour of many good things lost, perhaps irretrievably. Later in the same session Gillian lifted a restless Sam from the pushchair and gave him the breast; Sam sucked for a while, and Gillian said, in a rather resigned way, 'all he wants is titty'. Almost as if he wanted to contradict her, Sam let go of the breast shortly after and started sucking a piece of string which was hanging form the hood of his cardigan; I looked at him and smiled. Gillian took the string out of his mouth and said, in a very irritated way and in a loud voice, 'not that, idiot' and put the nipple back in his mouth. Sam produced a gargle of agreement and started sucking at the breast again. I remarked that when when Sam felt that his mother's attention was elsewhere as she was talking with me, just as perhaps my attention was elsewhere during the holidays, he had started sucking a piece of string which was not very nourishing. Gillian who was by then much calmer and by now used to my 'messages in code', asked me if I was by any chance talking about her smoking spliffs during the holiday.

Interestingly, Sam's breast-feeding resumed. He was totally weaned only when he was thirteen months old, quite a few months later. I hope that the containment offered to Gillian in her sessions has spared Sam the experience of being repeatedly used by his mother as a recipient of projections of her psychic pain.

Up to now I have been talking about the eyes as organs of projections, and about parents who project instead of containing, and of very alarming clinical situations, so I am going to conclude by providing some little relief. I will describe a very beautiful and touching sequence which took place when Gillian was still bringing Sam to her sessions. It is a sequence often seen in infant observations when it is clear that the eyes (in particular the attention of the mother) are like a magnet which holds a baby together and which reinforces his endoskeleton (Bick, 1971, verbal communication).

Sam was sitting on the carpet next to his mother's feet. He had tried three times to lift himself on his legs holding on to the side of the couch, but he had fallen back on the floor, fortunately very well protected by his nappy. Gillian had ignored him. I stopped talking and turned my glance towards Sam. Gillian also looked at him and smiled, saying rather affectionately, 'What a twit'. Sam looked at her, glued his eyes to her eyes and without any physical help lifted himself on his legs, hanging on to the eyes of Gillian. He smiled and looked very proud of himself.

9

The No-Entry System of Defences

Reflections on the Assessment of Adolescents Suffering from Eating Disorders

For some years I have been interested in work with patients who are difficult to reach, and patients with eating disorders do often belong to this category. In many of them I have experienced a quality of '*do not trespass*' that has brought me to formulate the hypothesis of a 'no-entry' system of defences. In this chapter I shall describe problems encountered in the assessment and treatment of an adolescent suffering from eating disorders where this 'no-entry' syndrome was unusually pervasive, and extend the theme of the child as recipient of parental projections from Chapter 8.

Sally was referred to the Adolescent Department of the Tavistock Clinic for the first time when she was seventeen, when the symptoms of her anorexia were extremely serious. When I met her for the first time in the waiting room, I found a young Afro-Caribbean girl wrapped up in an anorak, and felt she was somewhat swimming in it. She had very short hair, was wearing blue jeans and I could see how very thin her legs were; she wore masculine shoes. As I wrote in my notes, 'my initial feeling was one of having in front of me a very thin, twelve-year-old *boy*'. Sally had the earphones of a Walkman around her neck as she walked with me towards my room with rather quick and vigorous steps. At the beginning of the session she gave me the impression of holding herself together with a marked muscular tension, a sort of defensive 'armour' (Bick, 1968, p. 275), inside the wrapping of the enormous padded anorak which she didn't take off. Her thin face made me think of a frightened bird; it was pale, but did not have an agonising look.

The tension diminished a little when I told Sally that I realised that it was difficult to come to a new place to meet a new person. Maybe she was asking herself what I wanted to ask her and what I was going to tell her. When she became a little more relaxed Sally told me that everybody seemed to be 'breathing down her neck' because they said she was eating too little. Then she stopped speaking. I felt that she was clearly expecting me to ask her what she ate every day. I said I had the feeling that she didn't like it very much when people asked her questions, when people were 'breathing down her neck'. Sally said that what she ate was not so little after all, since she had some toast and some chocolate every day; however, she didn't tell me how much toast or how much chocolate it was (for all I knew it could have been half a toast and a square of chocolate). She said that she wasn't so thin and she told me her weight. Her mother was much, much thinner than herself, having gone down to 4 stone. At this point I asked Sally if she might wish to talk with me about her mother and said that she could talk about anything she liked.

Sally then started talking. I felt at times that she was wrapping herself in her words rather as she was wrapping herself in her very large anorak (Bick, ibid.). About her mother, Sally said that she used to eat next to nothing, maybe a piece of toast each day, but that she used to drink a great deal, that she was an alcoholic. Her mother died when she (Sally) was thirteen, she told me. At first she said that she died of kidney failure, then she corrected herself and said 'No, perhaps it was not her kidneys'. Anyhow, it was linked with her addiction to alcohol. Then Sally said, *without my putting any question to her*, that she was disgusted at the thought of alcohol as she didn't like losing control in any way. I felt at this point that she wanted to tell me that she was not addicted, she wasn't as ill as her mother. She might have anorexia in common with her but her mother did not die of anorexia, she died because of being an alcoholic. I realised later that she was telling me 'I am not in danger of dying. The addiction that killed my mother is not my addiction. I am not at risk, don't send me to hospital'. I would have opportunities later to understand more about the reasons for this defensive attitude, and about Sally's fear of being admitted to hospital where she would be tube fed in order to put on weight. Sally's mother had been admitted to hospital and tube fed more than once; she had also been admitted to hospital because of the 'alcohol problem', but this had really been 'of no use at all', according to Sally.

Sally experienced particular terror at the thought that she might be *tube fed*. It had never happened to her but she had heard about it from her mother, who had been very frightened by it and it was quite true that should she not have put on weight, which fortunately happened in the following months, she would have had to be admitted to hospital. Indeed, when Sally told me about her mother's terror at being tube fed, she also told me that her mother was almost always frightened unless she was very drunk. For instance, she was frightened of drowning in the bath tub and Sally had to hold her hand when she had a bath. I asked whether she remembered how old she was at the time when she started holding her mother's hand during a bath. Sally wasn't sure, maybe she was three or four. Then she said that she knew why her mother was so frightened; when she (her mother) was very little, she had almost been drowned by her own father (Sally's maternal grandfather), who had kept her head under the water and threatened his wife (Sally's maternal grandmother) that he would drown the little girl. This was during a violent marital row.

I commented that Sally seemed to be telling me that early experiences might leave a mark and I emphasised the fact that this was really what *she* told me. For I felt that this was the tiny amount of input which Sally could accept from me at that point without clenching her teeth. Sally then told me that she well remembered the violent rows between her parents before they separated when she was four; she remained with her mother while her two brothers went to live with father. Sally also went to live with father when mother died but she only remained with him from the age of thirteen to the age of sixteen. She had a difficult time with her father and with his new wife, and ran away from their house on the day of her sixteenth birthday.

Sally's mother had lost three children before Sally's birth, one being the twin of the eldest brother, and the three children had all died very young (cf. Reid, 1992). Sally heard from a neighbour that her brothers died because her mother did not take good care of them, and she didn't know if this was true. The same neighbour contacted Social Services when Sally was nine to let them know that the child was being grossly neglected. 'It was in fact true', Sally said, that 'my mother only fed me on some toast and that she spent all the money given by Social Services in order to buy her booze'. As a consequence of her contact with Social Services Sally spent about one uninterrupted year and subsequently some shorter periods in temporary fostering. In fact, I was to learn later that another reason for having been fostered at the age of nine was that Sally told a social worker that she had been sexually abused by one of her mother's partners.

The sexual abuse consisted in putting Sally's hands on the erect penis. Rather, Sally gave me to understand, in a very elusive way, that the man put her hand *on* his trousers; she shouted and he became frightened. Sally told me repeatedly during the assessment meetings that she felt a real disgust just at the thought of an erect penis which, she thought, she had never seen. She had always kept her head covered with a sheet when she shared mother's bedroom, she told me; Mother had many lovers.

Sally also told me that nobody had ever touched her genitals and that she hoped she would never see or touch a penis for the rest of her days; the expression of disgust on her face was reminiscent of somebody who was about to be sick. As Sally was talking about this I perceived in her the same emotional quality which I felt when she was speaking about her mother being tube fed: the terror of something 'breaking and entering' into her.

Sally's low weight meant that she had stopped having her periods. This frequently happens with anorexic girls who are often terrified about sexuality in general, but terrified of penetration in particular. In Sally's case, the 'no-entry' syndrome was very extended. She was frightened of being 'touched' on her skin; Sally had a very large number of soft, cuddly animals; she quite often slept hugging a teddy bear to which she had given a feminine name. She said she spoke to the teddy bear, especially when she had nightmares, and I asked her if she would be able to talk about one of these nightmares. She answered that there was a terrible dream which always came back, but she put across the feeling that she was not inclined to tell me more about it. On this occasion, I rather lightly said a sentence I would often repeat during our meetings, 'Do not trespass'. This sentence seemed to be on the right wavelength because Sally repeated my words, laughing, giving me the feeling that she felt understood.

The only doctor whom Sally was prepared to see when it was absolutely necessary was the one who had referred her to us. This woman doctor seemed to be capable of understanding Sally's dread of being touched and her psychopathology in general; we kept in touch with her about the literally *vital* issue of keeping an eye on Sally's weight. However, Sally had always managed to avoid going to the dentist and her mother had not been worried about it. During the period of fostering when she was about 10 years old and again during the period when she lived with her father between the age of thirteen and sixteen, she had allowed a dentist to 'mess about in her mouth'. In both cases, it was because of a dental abscess, and on those two occasions Sally had to be given gas and air before she could be given a local anaesthetic, as she was so frightened of injections. She said that had they not 'knocked her off' she would have wriggled and would have broken the needle. She asked me – it was one of the very few direct questions she put to me – how would they have taken this broken needle out had it broken inside her gum?

At this point, I felt that Sally was accessible enough for me to venture into an interpretation; I told her that I did not know which procedure would be used in order to remove a broken needle, but I felt that Sally was frightened something might have become encapsulated in her in spite of the many 'do not trespass' signs that she had put around herself, She was asking me to give her hope that she might somehow free herself from it. I told her that in a clinic like ours, we try to do this with words not gas and air. I was hoping we could help her and that she could improve without having to be admitted to hospital and without having to be tube-fed (another persecutory image of an intrusive foreign body).

At this point, I would like to say that when working with, or assessing, patients like Sally, where the 'no-entry' syndrome looms large, I find myself speaking in a quite soft tone of voice. I try to avoid incisive words, preferring to use a 'pastel' rather than a 'primary colour' type of language. So I probably gave Sally more help with the tone of my voice than with the actual content of my verbal communications, when I told her that we were not going to do anything similar to the dentist. In the same session I spoke with Sally about the fact that she had made clear to me that there were a number of things, like her nightmares, which she preferred not to talk about. I said this was understandable since (I reminded her) I was going to see her only four times – this was the third assessment session.

Sally remembered very well that we only had one session left. She indicated that she was prepared to accept the offer of therapy by asking if I could give her the name of the person who was going to see her after we concluded the assessment. I told her her name was Mrs L. Sally was obviously reassured by the fact that it was a woman and she seemed happy when I said that Mrs L would be able to see her three times a week.

With hindsight, I wonder whether Sally might not have committed herself more to her therapy if she had been offered initially two sessions or perhaps only one. I also feel that with patients suffering from eating disorders, the change of person between assessment and therapy can be an obstacle in the development of a trusting relationship. It happens even if the assessor has been very careful not to encourage the development of a transference relationship. The work with Mrs L continued for about six months, during which time Sally improved considerably as regards her anorexic symptoms; she acquired weight (over a stone) and was no longer in the 'at risk' category. However, as the long summer break approached, Sally started missing sessions. She refused to resume her sessions in September in spite of the repeated attempts of her therapist to get her to come back.

About 18 months after the interruption of the therapy Sally wrote to the Adolescent Department saying that she wished to see someone for some sessions (someone other than Mrs L). In fact it would have been impossible to see Mrs L because she no longer worked at the Tavistock. It was suggested in the assessment workshop that I gave an appointment to Sally, and I started seeing her for an open period of joint exploration. I knew at that point that I could offer her an open-ended commitment if that seemed desirable; I now think that it is easier for eating disorder patients to accept one session initially and gradually increase the number. In my view this is intimately related to the hypothesised 'no-entry' syndrome.

I will not speak at length about the changes I found in Sally's appearance, other than to say that she had became much more feminine. I was soon confronted with the presence of relevant 'no-entry' clusters which were still present in her pathology. However, her eating problems were much less alarming. She was still outside the 'at risk' category, thin but certainly not emaciated, and was controlling her food intake quite carefully and counting calories. Days of near-starvation therefore followed when she felt she had eaten too much.

In our joint exploration I made a direct link between Sally's concern with the amount of food and the amount of help she was prepared to take from me without feeling that I was 'breathing down her neck'. Our work acquired the texture and the feeling of a real 'joint exploration' when I told Sally that, should she proceed with therapy after the assessment, I would be able to see her myself. There would be no change. I also told her that it might be difficult for her to accept more than one weekly session. For my part I now felt much more comfortable. In the countertransference, I was less worried about the 'do not trespass' signs, feeling rather like a parent who puts a plate on the table: the child is free to take the food or not. Incidentally, I find that this image is often helpful in describing the technique of joint exploration with this type of patient.

In the third session of this second assessment Sally described to me the recurring nightmare she had mentioned in the *first* assessment. Perhaps she *was* worried that our contact might end after four sessions as it had happened before; telling me about the nightmare might have been an attempt to hold on to me. She had certainly decided she was going to talk about it between the second and the third session, because she said that she knew it would be difficult to describe the dream/nightmare and she had brought me a drawing she had done at home to give me a representation of it. The dream consisted of her feeling paralysed and invaded by a mass of tadpoles. The tadpoles penetrate all her orifices. From the drawing it was evident that the mouth was only one of the orifices concerned with this enormous flood of tadpoles.

The terror that these foreign bodies might enter the rectum and the vagina could be easily narrowed down to a fear of invasive spermatozoa but I think would also be limiting. Above all, the nightmare provides a concrete image of Sally's dread of being invaded and broken into while in a defenceless state. It is obviously also intimately related to Sally's anxiety about penetration, but I am talking about a much more pervasive dread of allowing *anything* to come inside, through whatever orifice. We are confronted with a massive confusion between orifices, but also with a pervasive anxiety which is not only due to such confusion; every access is a possible access to persecutors. Let me come back to something Sally had told me when I first met her: that her mother asked her, when she was very young, to hold her hand when she was having a bath because she was terrified of drowning. I see in this description a graphic image of a child used as a *receptacle* of projections of a parent's anxieties, anxieties which have not been metabolised/digested by the parent; the child has not as yet developed the equipment to digest and take this input into his or her own 'bloodstream'. I have purposefully used the word 'receptacle' and not the word 'container', as the word container implies a *capacity* for containment. I would like therefore to suggest that:

> *A pervasive symptomatology with a 'no-entry' quality can represent a defensive system developed by a child who has perceived himself/herself (early in infancy), to have been invaded by projections. These projections are likely to have been experienced by him or her as persecutory foreign bodies. The 'no-entry' syndrome performs the defensive function of blocking access to any input experienced as potentially intrusive and persecutory.*

In this way I will continue the exploration begun in Chapter 8.

The 'no-entry' system of defences can be limited and circumscribed at times, manifesting itself in some patients solely with anorexic symptoms. The case of Sally is in fact one of the most extreme examples of this type of symptomatology, for the 'no-entry' symptoms were not limited to anorexic ones. They were present in her fear of being tube fed, in her terror of the dentist, of injections, sexual penetration, of the telephone or the alarm bell ringing. The 'no-entry' symptoms were so pervasive that Sally was even frightened of being touched *on* her skin.

It is, however, possible that a projection of something which could not be digested did not start when Sally was three or four years old and after the parents separated. For it is difficult to imagine that a very ill mother, whom we know was not particularly supported by her husband, could have been able to work through the mourning of the three children she lost before Sally was born. Indeed, the similarity between the tadpoles and spermatozoa suggests that Sally's nightmare could also be related to a persecutory phantasy about dead babies, perhaps dead babies that the mother had not been able to mourn. As the tadpoles were described by Sally as devouring, they might also have had something to do with her own greed. This greed became much more evident during the work of therapy than it was during the period of assessment. However, the observations I am making about the nightmare of the tadpoles (dead-babies greed) are related more to material which emerged during the therapy, and do not belong either to the first or the second assessment stage; I will not enlarge on this subject as I am mainly focusing in this chapter on the issue of assessment.

I would just like to remark, in conclusion, that Bion spoke of 'nameless dread' when he was talking of the return of projections which have not been received, contained, metabolised, by the parental object, and I am sure that Sally had also had this experience of 'nameless dread'. However, I would like to suggest that the definition of *nameless dread* applies just as much to, and is the most appropriate definition I have found up to now for, the experience of a child when he or she is used as a *receptacle* of parental projections.

10

On Introjective Processes

The Hypothesis of an 'Omega Function'

In this chapter I am mainly relying on a Kleinian frame of reference and some concepts of Bion. Nevertheless, attempting to describe the theme of Chapter 10, I cannot think of a more beautiful image than the one provided by Freud in 'Mourning and Melancholia' (1917), when he spoke of the '*shadow* of the object falling upon the ego' and of the paraphrases of this sentence offered by Karl Abraham when speaking of the '*radiance* of the object' reflected upon the ego (1924); and which were called to mind in my treatment of Ingrid (see Chapter 5).

This play of lights and shadows in the quality of the internal objects acquires an almost tangible dimension in the description of the internal world and of the internal space which is central in the work of Klein. The existence of this internal space was implicitly present in the work of Freud: he spoke about the shadow of the *object*; this internal object must occupy an *internal space*. In the case of Schreber (Freud, 1911) he spoke of the external catastrophe being a mirror image of an *internal catastrophe*.

I shall begin with a description of introjective processes that is more related to the play of lights than to the play of shadows. First of all, I wish to talk of introjective processes which facilitate development. In the second part of this paper I will focus on particular types of introjective processes which *create an obstacle to development* and may bring about the introjection of an object performing a function which is the obverse of alpha function.

The Play of Lights

In 'Envy and Gratitude' (1957), Melanie Klein gave a very beautiful definition of the process which provides a connective tissue in the personality. The basis of a feeling of integration, of steadiness, of inner security, she writes, is the consequence of 'the introjection of an object who loves and protects the self and is loved and protected by the self'. Bion developed Klein's theory, stressing the *function* of this introjected object, which is essentially to make feelings thinkable, understandable and therefore tolerable. He describes how it is necessary for a healthy emotional development, to have the experience of a parental object (it is often the mother) who can receive a cluster of sensations, feelings and discomforts that the child cannot give a name to and is therefore unable to think about. The function of this object, defined by Bion as 'alpha function' or 'reverie', as we have seen, is the one of keeping in the mind, giving a meaning, making thinkable those feelings for the child also. It is necessary, in order to fulfil this function, that the parental object should be able to tolerate the psychic pain the child cannot tolerate himself. After repeated experiences of this containment, such a function can be internalised by the child as he grows up and he gradually becomes able to better deal with his anxiety within his own mental space.

In an international conference of Tavistock Model Courses on the theme of reparation, I was struck by the presentations of two child psychotherapists. The transference experience of their child patients put across very strikingly *their appreciation of being helped to think*. Nicoletta Lana (in Cosenza et al., 1995) spoke about Giorgio, a child who was born with a serious malformation of his diaphragm and had to be urgently operated immediately after his birth. In the first part of her paper, the therapist describes a confusion in Giorgio's internal world which was similar to the one present in his body at birth, where necessary boundaries were not yet defined. We followed through the development of the transference relationship, a process which brought Giorgio, who was ten years old at the time, to define his therapy as a 'workshop of thoughts' (*'officina di pensieri'*).

Next, the case of a child who had been severely physically abused by his mother when he was a baby and had been very close to death was presented by Rosemary Duffy (in Cosenza et al., 1995). She spoke about Daniel as being initially full of persecutory anxieties and extremely confused. For him as well, therapy gradually became a 'workshop of thoughts', but using seven-year-old Daniel's own words I will share with you the definition which he gave of one of the central concepts of Wilfred Bion's theory. This is Daniel speaking with his therapist. 'I know you were thinking just then. Sometimes when I see your face thinking, I am thinking too'. Later: 'I am thinking about joining a "thinking club"'. This same child asked his therapist 'Please, help me to think thoughts.' He certainly wished and was able, at this point, to be helped to think about 'where it hurts and why it hurts'.

I will now move from the therapeutic context to an observational one, always with specific reference to the introjection of an object which helps to think and negotiate difficult feelings but not, in this case, traumatic feelings. I will talk about a little girl, Julie, whom I have observed from birth. She was 19 months old at the time of the observation I'm going to quote.

Julie

Julie had had a massive tantrum because mother had prevented her from playing with a fragile object. She had become red in the face, had stamped her feet and had been, even if briefly, very intensively angry and upset. Mother took her on her lap and, initially, Julie pushed her away saying: 'go away, go away'. Julie had calmed down little by little while mother held her lovingly and spoke with a soft voice. She told her that she could play with something which would not break so easily. She offered her some plastic stacking beakers. At first Julie threw the beakers away, and mother picked them up and assembled them each inside the other. Then Julie, sitting on the floor, started a game with the beakers. She built a tower by putting them one on top of the other, knocked the tower off, built it again, and finally began to assemble them each inside the other. Mother kept talking with her saying that Julie had knocked the tower off but the beakers were not broken. Julie smiled to mother, repeating 'not broken'. Then she got up and picked up a doll called Poppy; it was one of her favourites from the time when she was very little. (I had seen her using it in previous games as a sort of alter-ego.) Julie took Poppy by the arm and shook her, making an angry sound. In fact the image of the doll having a tantrum was extremely realistic. Julie then put the doll on mother's lap, conveying very clearly the message that she wished for mother to make her better. Mother talked to the doll, then gave it back to Julie who started the sequence again, shaking the doll, then putting it on mother's lap. On the third occasion, Julie consoled the doll herself, repeating some fragments of mother's words. This sequence was repeated many times during this observation and it became more and more of a game.

It is of course difficult to observe the full texture of an introjective process while it is taking place in an observation. We have been able to see just a fragment, an episode of this slow process. It was necessary for Julie to repeat the sequence while working at it very seriously, even if I referred to it as a game. She was working at a differentiation between a part of herself overwhelmed by feelings of rage (represented by the doll), and a part which could observe and attempt to understand or even soothe those feelings just as her mother had done with her, not only then, but, repeatedly, in the preceding 19 months. One of the most meaningful aspects of this sequence is, in my view, the fact that Julie has initially put the doll on mother's lap for her to make it better, almost as if saying: 'you show me how to do it'. This attitude, with its component of admiration towards one's object, is very central to introjective processes that are favourable to development.

The Play of Shadows

I said at the beginning of the chapter that I was going to talk about lights and shadows. I have spoken of 'the play of lights', but now I would like to describe introjective processes that are much more in the area of shadows which not only do not facilitate development, but hinder it. Wilfred Bion described the process which takes place when the object is impervious and not open to receiving projections. Projections which have not been accepted return to the infant, as he says, as 'nameless dread'.

In my work with patients suffering from eating disorders, I have developed a particular interest in the *quality* of introjective processes and in particular in the introjection of a function I could refer to as a possible '*omega function*' in order to stress how its characteristic are at the opposite end of the spectrum from alpha function. 'Omega function' derives from the introjection of an object which is not only impervious, but is both impervious and overflowing with projections. Just as the introjection of alpha function is helpful in establishing links in organising a structure, the introjection of 'omega function' has the opposite effect, disrupting and fragmenting the development of personality.

This characteristic brings to mind comparatively recent developments in the field of attachment theory. Mary Main (Main and Solomon, 1990) has suggested that a fourth category of attachment pattern, namely the one of '*disorganised, disoriented attachment*' should be added to the three well-known categories (secure, ambivalent and avoidant). The children who developed 'disorganised, disoriented' types of attachment had been exposed to the experience of parents who had themselves suffered a trauma in their lives and were either *frightened* or *frightening* or both. From a psychoanalytic perspective, 'frightened or frightening' parents are those who *project anxiety instead of containing it.*

In order to clarify what I mean by 'omega function' it may be useful to give some short examples from two infant observations where external factors (not related to the psychopathology of the parents) created a situation where an infant was himself the *receptacle* of anxiety perceived by him as persecutory. The attempt to reject the introjection of this disorganising 'omega function' took the form of serious eating difficulties. In both cases it was impossible for the parental objects to contain projections of anxiety, in particular they could not contain *the infant's fear that he himself might die*, defined by Bion as the most crucial primitive anxiety. In both observations there was a very heavy cloud weighing on the parents. It was a cloud of mourning which had not been worked through or which was impossible to work through. Their state of mind made it difficult for them to accept the anxieties about the death of their child and instead they established a process which reinforced the infants' anxieties about death. Thus not only was the infant not himself contained, but he became the *receptacle* of parental projections. Both infants appeared to have introjected an object which can be seen as performing an 'omega function'.

Faruk and Patrick

Faruk was the child of Somali refugee parents; in the families of both parents, relatives had died because of war or famine. It was impossible to contact the surviving members because they were moving from one place to another in order to find food. There was no news from Somalia at the time when the child was referred to the paediatric department of a London hospital, because of serious feeding difficulties including food refusal and persistent vomiting. Fouzia, the mother, was almost certain that her father had died, but this was a loss of which she had no certainty, therefore she could not begin to mourn.

Faruk's symptoms were particularly meaningful as he was rejecting food in a family where many relatives had died of starvation. It increased the mother's anxieties about the baby's possible death even more. The fear that the child could die brought about frequent force-feeding; alternatively, Faruk was fed with the bottle whilst asleep. The family was followed with a 'participant observation' by a Tavistock/University of East London student, Mariangela Pinheiro (Pinheiro, 1993). From her observations we can see a number of elements supporting the hypothesis that a great deal of anxiety about death might have overflowed from the parents into the baby and that, at least to an extent, Faruk's rejection of food might have had the meaning of warding off the introjection of an overflowing object which could have a disorganising effect on his internal world.

In spite of this warding off, this literal 'rejection', there is evidence that some introjections of disruptive and disturbing elements had taken place. For instance, Faruk is described by the observer at the age of one year and two months as incapable of keeping his attention focused on a task for any length of time, as easily distractable, as being in a state of mindlessness and rather clumsy in the coordination needed to hold an object firmly. Fortunately, these less organised or even disorganised moments alternated with others where the child was more coordinated and had better cohesion.

An even more alarming case was described by the same 'participant observer' (Pinheiro, 1993). Patrick, a four-month-old baby, was originally referred to the paediatric department of a London hospital because of food refusal and spitting out both solid and liquid food. He had acquired minimum weight since birth, and in this case too, very heavy anxieties concerning death were weighing on the parents. Three children had been born before Patrick, all of them premature; they had died within a few hours after their birth. Patrick was also born prematurely and his mother refused to look at him during the first week because she was sure that he was 'another one to go'. The child's food refusal naturally increased the parent's anxieties in an exponential way, and this anxiety overflowed into Patrick. He tried to keep the projections at bay with a violent rejection, much more violent than the one that could be observed in Faruk. There was an improvement due to the help of the hospital where the child was admitted, as well as the help of the 'participant observer', but it was very difficult indeed to help the parents to deal with their panicky force-feeding of the child.

The image of the kitchen as a 'battlefield', littered with food thrown or spat on the furniture or on the floor by Patrick, described by the observer from a visit when Patrick was seven months old, provides a graphic image of a function which is disruptive, rather than integrative in the internal world. If we look at the vivid description of the kitchen in the observation of Patrick in the same way as we would look at a drawing in a child psychotherapy session, we see that an important contributory factor in the fragmentation of the internal world is due to the explosive rage experienced by the child who is not being offered containment, but is used instead as the receptacle of projections he cannot deal with.

I have used the term 'omega function' instead of 'minus alpha function' because I did not want to make a reference to Bion's negative grid. The projection of anxiety into an infant does not in itself, imply the presence of those elements of perversion of links, or false links, which characterise the negative grid. It creates an undesirable link, even a dangerous one, but not necessarily a perverse link. Indeed, I doubt that there was anything perverse in projections of anxiety about death into Faruk or Patrick.

Daniel

I shall conclude this chapter with a reference to another premature baby, a patient who is now an adolescent. Daniel was seriously bulimic and suicidal when he started therapy, and he told me that at birth he was the smallest baby in the county where his family lived. He had been in an incubator for over two months, and according to his mother, the doctor had given him up for lost. When Daniel was still in the incubator, his mother became pregnant with a 'replacement baby' who was born only eleven months after Daniel; had Daniel been born full term there would have been only eight months between them.

The lack of a containing space which could hold Daniel was very concrete in so far as he lost the space in mother's womb he would have still been entitled to. Additionally his mother, a woman who had herself been very severely deprived in her early infancy and suffered from severe psychotic symptoms, could not provide a receptive space for her children. During her frequent admissions to psychiatric hospital (the first one followed her attempt to set fire to the house), her children spent long periods in care. Daniel's father was an alcoholic who was addicted to hard drugs, and he could not look after the children either. Daniel had become anorexic like his mother at the age of fifteen, bulimic like her when he was eighteen.

I never met Daniel's mother, although I have some information about her as she was seen by a colleague at the Tavistock Clinic. She certainly suffers from severe psychopathology, and this significantly differentiates Daniel's case from the infants to whom I referred earlier. Daniel appears to have introjected, mainly through the relationship with his mother, an object that spills out chaos, disruption and anxiety into his internal world. This was very much in evidence at the time I started seeing him and when he was attempting to get rid of this disruptive agent through his bulimic symptoms. At the time when we started therapy, he binged and vomited up to six times a day and the sessions often made me feel flooded by material that was full of confusion and I had to struggle to make links.

My countertransference experience was however, very different from the one I had with patients who were determined to attack links. Daniel was very frightened that his projections could be lethal and that I would return them to him. I remember a letter he wrote to me after a Thursday session.

> I've only seen you today and I am already here writing. I am sure that you are sick of me. I have read almost every minute since our meeting. I have started reading Plato for my essay, then I remembered that I had not finished the Joyce book I was reading, so I left Plato and I started reading Joyce. It is now 11.00 at night. I have read a little bit of Plato, a little bit of Joyce, I have almost finished Wilde's amazing *Portrait of Dorian Gray*, but I can't remember very much about it. Then I started reading Plato again but I cannot stay with anything. If I could come to a session tomorrow, you could help me to find some rhyme or reason in what is happening.

There is undoubtedly a great deal of idealisation in this letter but also I think, a genuine wish to learn to take inside something that might stay; there is also an element of the 'please show me how to do it' that we saw in the relationship between baby Julie and her mother. One can also hear in his words the presence of an agent which creates anxiety and hear in his words the presence of an agent which creates anxiety and disruption, perhaps a disorganising 'omega function'. His random grabbing has shifted from food to literature, but still nothing stays inside. with areas of shadow in Daniel's internal world. I do not think that we can, as yet, talk about a *stable* introjection of alpha function which could help him with possible disruptive incursions of the omega function. However, from a descriptive point of view, there is now more 'rhyme and reason' in Daniel's life. He does not suffer from bulimic symptoms; he has passed some exams; he lives with his girlfriend, a Spanish student who, I think, has her feet firmly on the ground. The relationship with his mother is much less conflictual.

Let us return to the internal landscape. Within the scope of this chapter I cannot give you a detailed account of a session, but, just as I have described a game of the infant Julie in order to give a glimpse of her introjection of some aspects of her relationship with her mother, I will refer briefly to a dream of Daniel's; it has given me hope about the development of introjective processes. Daniel had to write an essay on the 'difference between knowledge and belief', and had had great difficulty in writing this essay. In his dream I spoke to him and told him that an act of faith was needed in our relationship because he had no certainty or knowledge about me. It seemed that this dream was related to something we had spoken about in connection with the forthcoming holiday and Daniel's feelings that he could have no certainty about me. He actually feared that I might be 'sick of him' and might not return.

There was no shade of ambivalence in the dream, and there was undoubtedly an element of idealisation. It was still very difficult for Daniel to tolerate the conflict of mixed feelings he experienced towards me. Nevertheless, the dream helped him to find some 'rhyme and reason' and to put his trust in his internal object. It helped him to write the essay on knowledge and belief before his subsequent session. My function in the dream, I think, was to help him to think about something painful concerning separation anxiety heightened by the forthcoming holiday. My role was to help him to think with me about 'where it hurts and why it hurts' and perhaps become more capable of tolerating psychic pain.

We see something similar in Julie's observation when she asks her mother to help her reintegrate her feelings of rage and frustration, but the central element in Daniel's dream concerns the psychic pain related to *loss* and *separation*. As we have seen, as Freud wrote in 'Mourning and Melancholia' (1917), if one does not work through the experience of loss, if there is a failure of this process whether one is dealing with actual loss or with separation, 'the shadow of the object falls upon the ego' (p.249). The observation of Faruk and Patrick has given us a picture of the shadow of this heavy cloud related to unmourned or unmournable losses.

A holiday of one week was not, in itself, a dramatic separation but it confronted Daniel with the challenge of thinking about someone absent and of keeping that person in mind as a good object. So the dream gives us some hope that introjective processes are beginning to take place which are likely to help Daniel in this direction. I hope that our work might help him to internalise what has been described, in the words of Klein already quoted (see page 70), as the basis of the sense of inner security: 'the introjection of an object 'who loves and protects the self and is loved and protected by the self' (Klein, 1957, p. 188).

11

Foreign Bodies

In this chapter I will describe, in much greater detail, work with the adolescent to whom I briefly referred in Chapter 10. Daniel was a patient who had remained extremely porous to parental projections and had not developed a protective 'no-entry system of defences' (cf. Chapter 9). You will remember that he was born severely premature and that his mother had given him up for lost: the doctors had told her that he would not survive.

It was necessary for a child so deprived, to establish some trust in me in the transference relationship, as a reliable container, before he could shift from controlling something inanimate, like food, or the books he 'devoured' ('always available *things*' which he never needed to wait for), and begin to develop a relationship of dependency on, rather than addiction to, another person, one who was by no means as available to his control as things inanimate.

In that he was born addicted to Valium, Daniel had had, from the very beginning, an experience of concrete foreign bodies seeping into his bloodstream. He was ten weeks premature and was born with a number of malformations, including an occlusion of his nasal tract (non-patent nostrils). You will remember that his mother had become pregnant again when he was still in the incubator. The baby was born a beautiful, normal child, Julian. Mother said that she could not look at Daniel when he was born since he was so deformed and she hated deformity.

Daniel is an attractive boy of average size whom I started seeing about four years ago, shortly after his eighteenth birthday. I shall focus mainly on a late period of treatment when I had increased his sessions from three to four per week and when the states of mind and the dynamics underlying the initial eating disorder became much clearer in the context of the transference relationship. Initially, I understood Daniel's need to control me, especially his engendering much anxiety in the countertransference with suicidal threats, as a form of omnipotence, akin to that of another very deprived child David (described in

Chapter 7), that is, as a form of primitive coercion, fulfilling a 'survival function' (Symington, 1985).

A dream of the early period of treatment conveyed, I felt, the expectation on Daniel's part, or at least his wish, to be held by me as if he were again a small infant. It was a particularly difficult time for him since his mother was probably again going to be admitted to psychiatric hospital and she was heavily projecting into him. *He dreamt that I picked him up as if he were a baby and I held him very firmly.* When he told me about this dream, he said that he knew that this was how he would have liked things to be. He would, for instance, have liked me to help him to 'find some rhyme and reason' (cf. Chapter 10) in his life project. He could not make up his mind about the subject he was going to read at university. I knew him well enough to make up his mind for him.

I could not take on the role of providing the maternal early containment that he had lacked. His expectation was similar to Martin's (cf. Chapter 3) that he be given in the present what he had missed out on in the past. Daniel needed to be helped to cope with the pain of realising that what he had not had as a small child needed to be mourned and could never be obliterated by constant and always available mothering; Martin's fantasy about 'the restaurant open at all hours of the day and night' (cf. Chapter 3). The shift to the stage of treatment I am going to describe in detail in this chapter involved an extremely painful process of renunciation.

As I said in the previous chapter, at times I experienced confusion in the countertransference. I did not perceive this confusion as a wish in Daniel to break links and to make it impossible for me to think (cf. Chapter 3, 'You think, you think you are a brain box') but rather as his need to find an object that could experience the confusion and still remain able to find 'some rhyme and reason'. I attempted to detoxify his experience of being pervaded by inimical foreign bodies so that he could gradually internalise the function of an object capable of 'making emotional sense' (Bion, 1962).

In the initial period of treatment it was difficult to differentiate a legitimate need for containment from an attempt to exercise control over me, which had a deathly and paralysing quality to it. I often fluctuated between feelings of being too soft and too strict in my transference interpretations and in my attitude. Daniel had not renounced attachment to his primary object as had Louise and Martin (Chapter 1 and Chapter 2), nor had he become entrenched in 'unholy alliances' like Pekka and Ingrid (Chapters 4 and 5). There were, however, some similarities with the very deprived patient, David, described in Chapter 6: a vigorous, albeit controlling, attachment to the object. He told me that his mother most of all valued his 'tenaciousness'. He had learned from a very early age to 'try ten times harder than anyone else'. His mother, he told me, would say proudly about him, 'My Daniel would run to that lamp-post and back for me if I asked him'. When he was still very little and spent periods of time in a children's home while mother was in psychiatric hospital, he had managed to learn to do up his shoe-laces. He felt it would please mother when she saw 'what a clever boy he was' (this was said with a touch of bitterness). His brothers just left their shoe-laces undone until someone came to help them.

Mother valued Daniel's academic achievements and he had always been very succesful in his studies. His brother Julian, who was much taller than him and had 'the shoulders of a boxer', had never bothered with his studies. He was going to end up 'a bricky with the *Sun* (newspaper) in his back pocket'.

When he was twelve, Daniel used to jog on the spot for ten minutes every morning in order to become fitter. There was nothing he could do about his shoulders and mother kept telling him that he had 'no shoulders'. I think Daniel felt that what his brother had firmly in his pocket was the *sun*-shine of mother's smile. Daniel had gone with her to see Julian play in matches and she kept telling people, 'That is my son', when 'these great big hands lifted up in the line-out and grabbed the ball before anyone else could catch it'.

In spite of trying ten times harder than anyone else, Daniel felt that he had been fighting a losing battle. 'Those great big hands' had grabbed mother away from him. No wonder that when he read Rousseau in his philosophy classes, he chose to write an essay on 'The Rights of the First Owner'. His ownership of mother's womb had been taken up, as you will remember by Julian, when his tenancy rights had not yet expired and he was still in the incubator.

In the initial period of the treatment, I felt that holiday breaks were experienced by Daniel as cruel, and always untimely, evictions. From the beginning he had tried desperately to please me, just as he had with his mother. He realised that he found it difficult to be really sincere because he was busy trying to find out what for me would be the Daniel who could 'tie his shoe-laces', and was often telling me things that, he felt, 'would go down well'. At times he would play down the extent of his 'getting sick' as he called it, when he was still severely bulimic. Hell broke loose and his shoe-laces remained undone at the time of breaks, expecially in the first year of treatment. His suicidal threats felt very genuine and I took them seriously providing emergency cover, which was fortunately never needed. Close to holiday breaks Daniel used his mother as a 'receptacle' (cf. Chapter 8) of his suicidal ideation. I was sorry for her when I heard that Daniel had, at the time of the first Christmas break, given her a present which he himself later felt was 'a nasty thing to do': it was a volume of poems by Sylvia Plath, who Daniel knew had committed suicide. 'Not the best present for somebody who had often attempted suicide herself and, more than once, at Christmas'.

It took a long time before Daniel could experience some feelings of compassion for his very ill mother. As he had felt so painfully neglected and projected into by her, she became the carrier of feelings which he was desperately trying to exempt me from, at the time when he made a strong bid for mutual idealisation.

A very frightening dream, in fact a nightmare, made it clear that I was perceived as the one who was projecting panic and 'foreign bodies' into him. Close to a holiday break he dreamt that:

> I was trying to persuade him to experience the 'thrills' of bungy jumping from a bridge. In the dream he ran away and found himself in the corridors of his primary school. He hid in a childrens' lavatory and stood on the seat hoping that his feet would not be visible through the gap (the cruel gap of my holiday?) under the door. He woke up in a cold sweat.

Holidays breaks became more tolerable for Daniel when he engaged, about one year after the beginning of treatment, in a very intense relationship with a young woman, Maria (mentioned in Chapter 10), a relationship which turned out not to be a flash-in-the-pan piece of acting out, since it still lasts after three years.

Daniel's bulimic symptoms gradually receded, but he would still at times, binge and be sick after a session, especially after the last session of the week. He would eat nothing before coming to the session, at 10 o'clock in the morning, so that he would really feel hungry when he left and would have 'something to look forward to'. After we had done some work on the striking interchangeability of time between time with me and food, the symptoms eventually disappeared. Daniel told me the 'trick didn't seem to work any longer'. He was angry with me about it and offered me a rather strained, computer-language joke, 'You are no longer jam sandwich compatible.

A few months after Daniel met Maria, he moved out of mother's flat to live with her. He was able to tell Maria 'what a pig he used to be' only when he felt that his bulimia was a thing of the past. The bulimic symptoms did not return but Daniel was to tell me later in treatment with an element on nostalgia, 'Before you cured me of "getting sick" [his words for bulimia] at least I knew exactly what was going to happen every day'. On another occasion he was very openly angry: what was I doing to him? 'I have spent all my life trying to avoid anything to do with relationships and thinking about food instead. It is such a bliss to feel a longing for a bar of chocolate. You have just got to walk to the corner shop and your longing is assuaged'.

I do not think, as I said earlier, that Daniel had actually 'spent all his life trying to avoid anything to do with relationships'. I believe that he 'would have run to the lamp-post and back' if his mother asked him, but an iron grip of mutual control was present in that relationship.

Possessiveness

Daniel became increasingly aware that his current relationships, especially the one with his girlfriend, were pervaded by a spasmodic control akin to the one he previously exercised on food. He said that he knew of no other way of being with someone than 'merging with a person, which is a sort of devouring'. At times he saw his girlfriend as possessive. He said he accepted her being away 'very lightly'. He was not prepared to roll in guilt if he was not at home when she expected him to be there. On other occasions he was very much in touch with *his* possessiveness. He could not understand how Maria could put up with it: 'It must be hell to live with me. I cannot tolerate Maria liking anything I don't like. For instance, she might sit looking at a soap opera and I feel I could kill her because I hate soap operas'.

One day he became absolutely incensed when Maria was talking Spanish at home with a cousin of hers. He left the flat slamming the door. He said she was speaking a 'bloody language' which he could not understand and that she was also laughing and being cheerful. She should only be cheerful when she was with him. She had made him feel like a 'dysfunctional creep'. It was obvious that he felt incensed about my speaking a 'bloody language' which he could not understand with someone else when I escaped his control.

The possessive part of him became split off into a girl at college called Tanya. She was so clinging that people would prefer not to start talking to her because she would then complain when they went away. If somebody gave her attention but then said, 'Now I must go', she would moan: 'You never have time for me, I obviously bore you'. He criticised

Tanya fiercely and had great difficulty in the session in seeing her as a split-off part of himself. A dream came to our help.

> He was in an adventure playground and there were no adults about. Children were being cruel to one another. Tanya hit him hard in the legs. He fell but managed to get up again. No-one was there to protect him.

No parents were around to protect him from the pain engendered by this extremely possessive part of him that disturbed his balance (hit him in the legs). He said, 'What a quiet life I used to have when I was just thinking about food'. Daniel felt that he had become even more possessive since I had 'made him an offer he could not refuse', and increased his sessions to four per week.

Perhaps I was also felt to be very possessive. Some light was thrown on the 'plans' he felt I had for him in a session close to the dream of Tanya. He told me that he always used to try to win mother's attention by boasting, for instance, saying that he had scored a goal in football when in fact he had not scored a goal at all. I wondered what he thought was the goal he had to score for me, what he thought was my goal, my aim in making him an offer that he could not refuse. Daniel was silent for a short while and then said that my goal was to get him to admit that he feels jealous. Again, as in the old times, he felt that I pushed (projected) this unwanted jealousy into him, rather than putting him in touch with *his own* feelings of jealousy. Daniel also felt provoked by the increase in the number of sessions because his last one was on a Thursday. He said that now the 'weekend felt like a year long'. He referred to the week as four days of bingeing and the weekend as four days of starvation. During one of these 'year-long weekends' he had felt very hungry and thought he might have to start bingeing again, but felt that he could not do it any longer. He had not done it for a long time and 'it would really be a kick in the teeth to you and to Maria'.

This greedy part of him was split off in another dream:

> He dreamt that he was in a supermarket and a man was very angry with his son, a young boy, because the boy was taking loads of food off the shelf and the trolley was already full. Daniel persuaded the boy to leave the supermarket with him in order to escape his father's wrath.

The *father* was obviously experienced at the time as very persecutory. Daniel felt that the boy would be punished because of scooping food from the shelves which he could see, at this time, had something to do with what he had, in a previous session, called his 'voracious possessiveness'. Daniel told me that he felt that his hunger had the meaning of 'grasping for something outside'. 'If only I could have something inside I could hold onto, this would alter everything.' He also said: 'I could let go of somebody or something if I could believe that it would not disappear forever. If I could do that, a part of me which is organised and capable of pleasure could stay alive'. He also said that he had read somewhere that 'life is what happens when you are making other plans'. He referred to his 'consuming passion for making schedules', not very different from the way he was controlling his diet when he stopped bingeing.

He knew he *had* to plan the schedule of his days very carefully, and he resented the one day in the week when I was seeing him at a different time because it threw the schedule into chaos, two sessions were so close to one another and then there was a long gap.

Daniel had become aware by this time, that his preoccupation with his diet had only changed its target, but 'food doesn't mind if you keep it under control', while he felt it 'couldn't be fun' for me to deal with somebody *so* controlling.

He was to quote a poem about a butterfly saying that a butterfly, when caught in a net, loses its beauty. Daniel tried to understand the origin of his 'spasmodic control'. Could it have something to do with the fact that he never knew where he was with his mother? 'She had fits of rage and happiness that hit you like a thunderbolt from minute to minute'. He felt that I could not possibly imagine how controlling *she* could be.

For a short time, in between changes of flats, he went to live at mother's flat with his girlfriend. Mother 'took it on herself' to wash and iron Maria's clothes. She also 'took it on herself' to throw away some of Maria's underwear, which she thought was no good any longer, as well as some of Daniel's clothes which she did not like. 'I have to like my clothes, not my mother.' Daniel resented his mother buying clothes for him all the time. This was her way of keeping 'remote control' on him after he had left home. He resented her 'patronage', felt that she was buying things for him in order to 'own a part of me' (my offer of a fourth session?). If Maria bought him a new pair of jeans, mother had to buy him a better pair of jeans. 'It could be lucrative if it weren't so scary!'

Daniel said that he hated being controlled but that he knew that he was himself a 'control freak', just like his mother. It was 'frightening to see all these things she had shoved into him'. He used to think it was only the 'food problem', but now he felt he was perhaps 'just like her in so many other ways'.

Foreign Bodies from a Distance

Daniel became particularly aware of his tendency to enter into someone else's shoes (enter into projective identification) when his youngest brother Tommy began to develop a very familiar eating disorder. There was a great risk at this time of his trying to become 'me' by taking on a therapeutic role in order to intercept mother's projections into his brother. Daniel felt that what had happened to him was happening all over again. He knew 'the story inside out'. Mother had phoned him in tears saying, 'Daniel what shall I do'. She said that Tommy was now bingeing and vomiting, 'Just like you used to do' and that a friend of hers had told her that she reminded her of the song called 'My Life is a Circle'.

Daniel had tried to make light of things, telling his mother that if she did not give too much importance to what Tommy was doing and didn't bother too much with what he was eating, things would improve. Then he added, 'It is true that her life is a circle. It is happening all over again'. Tommy had started, just like Daniel, by becoming frightened of being too fat. He went swimming, he went to the gym, he exercised a great deal, looked at himself in the mirror and said that he was ugly. When Daniel spoke with him, he realised that Tommy had gone through a period of near-anorexia, just like he did. Mother had not been so worried at the time. Daniel remembered how she carefully planned his diet when he had gone down to 41 kilos and how she kept telling him that he should not become too fat. Daniel's mother said that people only become anorexic because of the influence of mass media. 'She should listen to *herself*, when she talks about people, she only comments on their appearance and whether they are fat or thin, never on their character. Mother really hated fat people and would die before she allowed Tommy to become fat.' Mother had told Daniel again on the telephone and in tears, that she had stopped buying biscuits and sweets and all the sort of things Tommy could binge on. Daniel felt like shouting at her, 'If you want to help Tommy just look at yourself. You only peck at food. You are frightened of it'.

In some detail, Daniel reported an outing with his brother when they had gone to the cinema, to see *Shine*. Daniel had cried looking at the film because he felt that he was himself just as trapped and imprisoned as the main character, only he was not a talented musician. He had 'no marketable skills'. Tommy had not noticed that Daniel was crying. Daniel had done his best to be cheerful. Tommy wanted to go to McDonald's and he had made the mistake of agreeing. Tommy had binged on junk food and when Daniel took him back home he had obviously gone to the toilet to be sick. Mother was aware of it. She was crying profusely saying, 'What do I do to my children?' Daniel felt that she was really only sorry for herself and that she was unable to be sorry for anyone else. They could hear that Tommy was in the kitchen bingeing on something and then he came into the living room and asked mother whether he could have a cup of tea. Mother shouted at him, just as she used to shout at Daniel, that if Tommy went on like that she was going to kill herself. Daniel was crying in the session when he told me about these events and he said that he really felt that he was not up to the task, that during the weekend he had somehow 'tried to be me'. 'Mind you', he added, 'If I have to become someone else because I am not as yet sure who Daniel is, I could do a lot worse than becoming you, much better than becoming Yvonne' (when he wanted to keep a distance from his mother he, at times, called her by her first name).

I spoke rather lightly about his 'becoming me' perhaps in order not to miss me as he had probably felt it might have beeen helpful to have a session at the weekend, when he was confronted with such an upheaval. Daniel regained some good humour and said with a half laugh, 'You have really got to start worrying when I begin to speak with a foreign accent'.

A Better Couple-Mixed Feelings

Daniel was very resentful of his girlfriend's attitude towards his mother. Maria, he said, 'did not mince her words'. She would say that Daniel's mother was completely crazy and the most irresponsible person she had ever met; she should never have been allowed to have children (perhaps irresponsible people like me, who kept taking holidays, should not be allowed to treat patients). She could not bear his mother's vulgar laughter; her talking in a 'garrulous' way with a thick northern accent, expecially when she did not have an axe to grind.

According to Maria, Daniel should stop meddling with the affairs of his family. When Tommy was developing his bulimia and Daniel was asked to perform some sort of protective role, she was frightened that he might get sucked back into a vortex at the time. 'She feels that it is dangerous for me and that you should tell me to keep away from Jakarta Road' (the street where mother and Tommy lived). Daniel said, with a mixture of envy and admiration, that Maria had certainly had a much better deal as far as her parents were concerned. He had met Maria's parents when he had spent a holiday with them. He had felt very welcome and had appreciated the fact that they tried hard to speak English most of the time in order not to make him feel excluded. Maria's mother had resumed her studies and had taken a new degree in her forties. Maria's father was a very educated man, a doctor. No wonder Maria always managed to keep her head above water, he said. She's got parents she could talk with if she was in trouble ('Well, now I have got you') and they seemed to have so much to give, probably because they give so much to one another.

I felt that this remark conveyed a deep insight into the real meaning of 'love-making' as *making*, producing something called love which can then be given to the children. He could experience admiration but he also bitterly resented having had parents so different from Maria's and always feeling at risk of going on 'automatic pilot' and becoming like one or the other of them, if not both.

There were some grounds to his anxiety because, in my clinical experience, I have often observed that the fate of foreign bodies frequently takes the path of an identification. A patient may indeed end up by identifying with an internal object perceived as a foreign body that he dreads or even, at times, hates.

Daniel started reminiscing about the good parent figures whom he had come across in his life, for instance, an aunt and uncle of his who had 'a real family', a family where they had regular meal times. There had never been such a thing in his family. He could not even remember Sunday lunches. Mother made a point, on occasion, of cooking a Christmas dinner, or 'her version of a Christmas dinner', but Christmas was often such an awful day as father would be out at the pub and came home drunk.

There had been important teachers in his school life. He remembered very vividly one from his primary school, Mr Richards, who could be both firm and gentle. There was a teacher in his secondary school who obviously taught English because he liked his subject. In this teacher's lessons, Daniel could just stay with one paragraph and not feel that he had to 'devour ten books'. He could savour his reading and he remembered feeling 'a warm glow inside' when he could savour literature instead of bingeing on reading. He spoke about this teacher as 'having a big imposing presence' and being quite firm with students who didn't do their work properly. He remembered in particular, a spoiled middle-class boy who dressed down and had his nose pierced in order to pretend that he was working-class and never did any work. He did not get away with any nonsense with the teacher who had 'the big imposing presence'.

The perception of a better couple stirred up mixed feelings in Daniel when it came to be anchored to the transference relationship. An event contributed to the welling up of tremendous rage in Daniel.

Mother was unwell and unfit to take care of her cleaning jobs (she had always worked as a cleaner). She had asked Daniel and Maria if they might wish to earn some extra money by taking care of the cleaning of a house in north-west London, where she generally used to work. The house was not far from the Tavistock Clinic. Daniel and Maria had accepted the offer as they were very short of money on their grant. They got the keys of this 'elegant house, not luxurious, but really tasteful'. It was 'full of books and classical music compact discs'. It belonged to a professional couple. The husband worked at home. He was a journalist, a tall, grey-haired, handsome man, 'educated and affluent'. Daniel imagined that this could be just the sort of husband I might have. He observed that there were a number of pictures of the couple's children; one of them was a graduation picture. Daniel was sure that it was 'graduation in some some prestigious university'.

Daniel felt provoked, as if I had deliberately goaded him by allowing him to have access to my home premises. I was again perceived as a *projecting* object. At this time Daniel noticed *for the first time* on the blackboard on the ground floor at the Tavistock that my name and the number of my room were next to two seminars, one on a Wednesday and one on a Thursday. One of the seminars took place only a quarter of an hour after the end of one of his sessions. 'How marginal' he was, how quickly I could forget about him and turn my mind to a seminar. He was sure that I had favourites amongst my students. Just like a teacher, whom he did not remember very fondly, who divided the students amongst the 'talents' and 'the others'. He was lucky because he happened to be one of 'the talents'. He was sure I had my favourites amongst my students and amongst my patients and he did not feel that he was one of the 'talents' – even if, at times, he did believe that I accepted him unconditionally, not because of the progress he made.

The image of the grey-haired, educated, affluent journalist merged with that of some politicians whom Daniel had heard delivering 'glib speeches' on television. Tony Blair was talking about a new era. There was going to be no 'new era' for Daniel. 'One should just become like one of them (the politicians) in order to have what they have got, the things so many people go without because others have got them.' The reference to what he felt I was giving to others: my partner, my favourites, the 'talents', my children attending prestigious universities when he has 'to go without', was very transparent.

At this time Daniel had a dream which left little doubt about his murderous feelings towards a hated couple. The dream took place close to a holiday break.

> Daniel dreamt that he had murdered the couple and he thought they were probably foreign tourists. He had murdered them on the shore of a cold barren island. Two policemen had got hold of him and he was sure they were going to beat him.

He woke up very frightened and got into a frenzy of tidying up. He felt that the bedroom was terribly messy while there were only Maria's and his clothes on the floor.

As I tried to understand the possible meaning of the 'foreign couple', Daniel associated the 'bloody mess' in the dream with a programme he had seen recently on television about present-day xenophobia in Germany. I was sure the xenophobia had, at this stage, something to do with my being foreign. (This attribute had been perceived by Daniel at other times as reassuring, since it meant that he could never really feel that he 'was me', that he could 'merge' with me.) The most violent feelings were directed, I felt, towards that unbearable 'foreign body' in my life, the 'third one' (Britton, 1989). A new and, hopefully, less toxic version of the dreaded 'foreign bodies'.

As I tried to explore the meaning of the dream, I wandered about the barren island. Why 'barren'? Daniel remembered he had countless times read two poems by Sylvia Plath: *The Barren Woman* and *The Pregnant Woman*. It was clear that murderous rage was also related to the grievance mentioned earlier in the paper, the hated pregnant mother-woman, who should have remained 'barren' and respected Daniel's 'rights of the first owner' to her womb, while instead, she had become pregnant with Julian when he, Daniel, was still in the incubator.

Talking about the 'bloody' mess in the dream, Daniel also remembered the 'bloody' mess in his parents' flat when father used to beat mother and she had more than once to be admitted to casualty. He said that if he could have dreams of this sort, he obviously had something ferocious and violent, something like his father, in himself. Daniel felt that 'he was not fit for human consumption'. He was unable for a time to make love to Maria because he feared he could be violent to her, that there was 'a beast' in him. He was furious with Maria when he got into

one of his 'savage moods' and she would just find him 'cute'. I wondered
whether he felt that I was perhaps going to find him 'cute' when he went
about murdering couples on the shore of a 'barren island', and when he
let me know about his 'xenophobia'. Daniel said, 'yes', he did not think
that I really knew 'what a savage' I had on my couch. I would only know
what a beast he could be if I had observed him bingeing. How he could
'demolish food' in such a way that not surprisingly he felt he had
immediately to make himself sick.

This was the first time Daniel so openly associated his bulimia with
a ferocious attack (perhaps breaking and entering into an impervious
object?). He was not far from seeing that it could be a ferocious attack
on mother's body, or the inside of mother's body, probably represented
by the supermarket in the dream previously quoted.

Projections of Jealousy and Abandonment

There was unfortunately, during an analytic break, some acting out of
Daniel's Oedipal jealousy. He became infatuated with a girl at college
and left around a diary in which he said that he felt attracted to this girl,
Caroline. Maria had read the diary and had cried profusely. Daniel
resented most of all that, in spite of feeling so hurt, she would have him
back. She should have told him, 'Go away then. If you have got
someone else on your mind, I don't want you'. Daniel felt that Maria
accepted him unconditionally even if he hurt her. She reminded him of
his mother who would always have his father back, no matter how
violent he had been with her.

He decided that he should leave Maria because he didn't want her
to be the victim of the savage in him. It took him a time, once we
resumed work, to realise that he had been savage in projecting all the
jealousy and the feelings of abandonment he was perceiving in the
transference relationship, into Maria. His abandonment of her was not
very dissimilar to something we had spoken about just before the
holiday. He had told me that he intended to drop the subject taught by
someone who was going to take an inordinately long break to go to his
country of origin in Latin America. The 'schedule' was going to be
messed up. Lessons at different times, a different teacher. I had spoken
about some veiled threat of wanting to 'drop' our subject, our work,
because of my forever going away and again messing up his 'schedule'.

Fortunately Maria did not take Daniel's threats of abandonment
'lying on her back' in the way that Daniel felt his mother had always
accepted his father's obnoxious behaviour. Maria had told Daniel at the

height of a rage: 'You can leave me and I'll be in a state for a while, but I will recover and get on with my life, while if you leave me you are going to be a wreck and remain a wreck for the rest of your life'. She also said: 'You feel you can do anything to me because at times I have said that I need you, but you never have the courage to say that you need anybody. That's why you are in the mess you are in'.

Daniel began to feel some genuine remorse about the feelings of abandonment he had inflicted on Maria. *It was true* that he had always tried to keep aloof. He remembered having mocked a friend of his who had been crying for three days, some years back, when his girlfriend left him. Daniel had told him that one should never let people know how much you like them.

He seemed to feel that once I had reached my 'goal' and he had let me know that analysis was important for him, I would say 'mission accomplished' and I would drop him. He said that he was not frightened any longer to use the words, 'I need you'. He said he knew he needed his sessions. At times he felt that he simply put his head down and made a dash for the next session. That's what made holiday breaks and weekends so difficult. His trouble was that when he needed something or somebody he wished to have them always available and he would like 'things to last forever'.

Once Daniel stopped projecting jealousy into Maria he at times experienced intense jealousy and envy in the transference relationship. On one occasion he told me that he had followed some teenage girls as they were coming out of a 'prestigious school' very close to the Tavistock. He had walked so close to them that he could hear what they were talking about. At first he was very derogatory, saying that they were just chatting and giggling like geese and what they seemed to be talking about was how early or how late they were allowed to return home. We knew from the time of his visit to the house in north-west London that he was certain in his mind that my children, the children who had been fathered by my attractive grey-haired, educated and affluent husband, had certainly attended prestigious schools and were probably now attending prestigious universities. He could see that his 'jaundiced eavesdropping' on the girls chatting had something to do with my privileged children.

The issue of being given a time to return home brought us back in touch with a subject that had emerged on previous occasions, for instance when he told me that there was never a meal time in his family. Indeed, he said, there was also never a time set for him to get back home. He would be playing in the street and all the children would be called back home for supper but he could stay out until well after dark, nobody would bother. Only occasionally, when father decided to stop drinking, generally for a week at the most, he would become extremely strict and set a bedtime for his children at 7.30 pm in the middle of the summer. Daniel remembered having to go to bed and hearing children still playing outside in the long summer evenings.

It was true he envied children who had parents who could set bedtimes and mealtimes. He was sure that was the way Maria had been brought up. He was in touch with his wish for the presence of a reliable paternal function, by contrast with his natural father. But he could also see that this was the same 'function' that brought about the end of sessions after exactly 50 minutes, which gave him firm holiday dates and firm session times and which established that he was not free to choose at what time of the day he could come to see me. He became keenly aware at this time of the conflict between the need for a reliable parental couple and the ambivalent feeling that this engendered. Such feelings were very clearly expressed in a dream such as the one of the murder on the shore of the barren island.

As Daniel gradually became aware that I was both someone he valued and someone whom he could passionately hate, he became more able to preserve contact with me in between sessions and also during breaks. He said that he did not feel any longer that he 'totally lost touch with me'. I think I was more 'together' in his mind and he often used this word when he said that whatever happened I always seemed to 'keep my cool'. I was at times so 'infuriatingly together'.

Some Shift in the Direction of the Depressive Position

At a time not far from a recent summer holiday break, Daniel came to his session saying that he had really made an effort not to be 'self-centred like his mother' and to help his girlfriend because she was in a state. She had not passed an exam for which she had worked very hard and she felt very upset indeed. Maria had taken out her rage on Daniel. She had accused him of being self-centred saying that she felt *so* neglected. She was screaming and crying and Daniel felt that she was really trying to say 'all the most hurtful things'. She had said for instance, 'You can go to your sessions and let things out – you have got someone you can talk-to. In the past you used to stuff yourself and throw up and now you can go and throw up all your troubles at the Tavistock'. Daniel had felt very tempted to deliver a little speech to Maria saying that his sessions had nothing to do with throwing up, but with his attempt to become a better person. Instead of saying so, he had tried to 'be a better person'. He had tried to 'keep his cool' and he was surprised because he had actually managed to 'feel together'.

He had told Maria that she could take the exam again and it was not the end of the world. He remembered how many times he had come to a session feeling that it was 'big drama', and by the time the session ended, it didn't feel any longer like the end of the world, it just felt like the end of the session. Daniel thought that he had perhaps felt so 'together' because Maria was 'in bits', but she had been grateful to him and told him, in the evening, that he had really been helpful 'for a change'. They had gone out for a Chinese meal and they had a lovely evening and a lovely night – lovely night was said with an element of innuendo.

Maria soon regained her good humour and Daniel told me on one occasion that she had helped him to make fun of himself and of his need for tidiness by imitating his voice: 'Oh – don't you know what those wardrobes are for – always leaving your things around'. Daniel said he had become aware of the fact that he had a tendency to assign roles to people just as his mother used to do. He had decided he was going to be the tidy one and Maria the messy one. He was now trying not to get into 'frenzies of tidying up' and was surprised to see that Maria was actually perfectly capable of taking on the task herself and she was not so messy after all. She was just not a 'control freak'.

I tried to figure out in what respect Daniel might have also implemented a role assignment within our relationship. As we were approaching a holiday break, I said that I felt that, although we both knew holiday breaks were worth thinking about, he seemed to have assigned to me the role of talking about them in advance, as if he felt that that was, perhaps, part of my 'script'. Daniel said I really had a point there and told me it was strange that I should mention that because, in the morning, he had been thinking that before the break started, we should 'draw the map of the minefield together'. It was true that he always left that job to me. 'Maybe', he said, and the joke felt a little strained, he could try to learn my lines and to be my understudy. Then he added: 'I know I need to make a joke of it because it *is* important'. There was still a risk that when the holiday started he might make a dash for the first book on the reading list for next year at college or get himself again into some 'passion for schedules'. Yes – he knew it was because he was so obviously completely out of control of my schedule, of my coming and going.

I will conclude this chapter with a verse Daniel quoted, reminiscing about the time when he felt he would never miss anybody because there was 'plenty of food in the supermarkets and the libraries were full of books'. He was aware that something had changed in him from that time, because a verse he had read some days previously had left a really deep impression on him.

The verse was: 'What you really love remains, the rest is dross'.

Bibliography

Abraham, K. (1924) 'A short study of the development of the libido, viewed in the light of mental disorders', in *Selected Papers on Psycho-Analysis*. London: Hogarth Press.

Bick, E. (1964) 'Notes on infant observation in psychoanalytic training', *International Journal of Psychoanalysis*, 45: 558-566.

—— (1968) 'The experience of the skin in early object relations', *International Journal of Psychoanalysis*, 49: 484-486.

—— (1971) Verbal communication.

Bion, W.R. (1957) 'Differentiation of the psychotic from the non-psychotic personalities', *International Journal of Psycho-Analysis*, 38: 266-75.

—— (1959) 'Attacks on Linking', *International Journal of Psycho-Analysis*, 40: 308-315, and also in *Second Thoughts*, London: Heinemann.

—— (1962) *Learning from Experience*. London: Heinemann.

Boston, M. (1967) 'Some effects of external circumstances on the inner experience of two child patients', *Journal of Child Psychotherapy*, vol.2, no.1: 20-32.

—— (1972) 'Psychotherapy with a boy from a children's home', *Journal of Child Psychotherapy*, vol.3, no.2: 53-67.

Britton, R. (1989) 'The missing link: parental sexuality and the Oedipus complex', in Britton et al., *The Oedipus Complex Today*. London: Karnac.

Cosenza, A., Monteleone, M. and Williams, G. eds. (1995) *La Riparazione: Storie di bambini alla ricerca di una officina di pensieri*. Pisa: il Cerro.

Freud, S. (1909) 'Notes upon a case of obsessional neurosis', *Standard edition of the Complete Psychological Works of Sigmund Freud*, vol.10. London: Hogarth Press.

—— (1911) 'Psychoanalytical Notes on an Autobiographical Account of a Case of Paranoia (Dementia Paranoides)', S.E. 11. London: Hogarth Press.

—— (1917) 'Mourning and Melancholia', S.E. 14. London: Hogarth Press.

—— (1920) 'Beyond the Pleasure Principle', S.E.18. London: Hogarth Press.

—— (1923) 'The Ego and the Id', S.E.19. London: Hogarth Press.

—— (1938) 'Splitting of the Ego in the Process of Defence'. S.E.23, London: Hogarth Press.

Henry [Williams], G. (1969) 'Some aspects of projective mechanisms in the Jungian theory', *Journal of Child Psychotherapy*, vol.2, no.3: 43-56.

Joseph, B. (1982) 'Addiction to near-death', *International Journal of Psycho-Analysis*, 63: 449-56.

Keats, J. 'Ode to a Nightingale', in *Keats: The Complete Poems*: 523-532. London: Longman.

Klein, M. (1946) 'Notes on some schizoid mechanisms', in *The Writings of Melanie Klein*, vol.3, *Envy and Gratitude and Other Works*. London: Hogarth Press.

——— (1952) 'The emotional life of the infant' in *Envy and Gratitude and Other Works*, London: Hogarth Press.

——— (1955) 'On Identification', in *The Writings of Melanie Klein*, vol. 3. London: Hogarth Press.

——— (1957) 'Envy and Gratitude', in *The Writings of Melanie Klein*, vol.3. London: Hogarth Press.

——— (1958) 'On the development of mental functioning', in *The Writings of Melanie Klein*, vol. 3. London: Hogarth Press.

Laplanche, J. and Pantalis, J.B. (1980) *The Language of Psycho-Analysis*. London: Hogarth Press.

Mack Brunswick, R. (1928) 'A Supplement to Freud's "History of an Infantile Neurosis" ', *International Journal of Psycho-Analysis*, 9: 439-469.

Main, M. and Hesse, E. (1990) 'Parents' unresolved traumatic experiences are related to infant disorganized attachment status: Is frightened and/or frightening parental behaviour the linking mechanism?' in M. T. Greenberg, D. Cicchetti and E.M. Cummings, eds., *Attachment in the preschool years*: 161-185. Chicago: University of Chicago Press.

Main, M. and Solomon, J. (1990) 'Procedures for identifying infants as disorganized/disoriented during the Ainsworth strange situation', in M. T. Greenberg, D. Cicchetti and E.M. Cummings, eds., *Attachment in the preschool years*: 121-161. Chicago: University of Chicago Press.

Meltzer, D. (1967) *The Psychoanalytic Process*. London: Heinemann.

Meltzer, D. et al (1975) *Explorations in Autism*. Perthshire: Clunie Press.

Meltzer, D. (1978) *The Kleinian Development*. Perthshire: Clunie Press.

——— (1979) 'Terror, Persecution and Dread', in *Sexual States of Mind*: 99-106. Perthshire: Clunie Press.

——— (1982) *The Claustrum*. London: Clunie Press.

Pinheiro, M.A. (1993) 'A clinical study of early feeding difficulties: risk and resilience in early mismatches within parent-infant relationship'. London: Tavistock Clinic, 1993 (MA in Psychoanalytic Observational Studies).

Potamianou, A. (1997) *Hope: A Shield in the Economy of Borderline States*. London: Routledge.

Reid, M. (1992) 'Joshua – Life after death. The replacement child', *Journal of Child Psychotherapy*, 18 no.2: 109-138.

Rosenfeld, H. (1971) 'A clinical approach to the psychoanalytical theory of the life and death instincts: an investigation into the aggressive aspects of narcissism', *International Journal of Psycho-Analysis*, 52: 169-178.

Shuttleworth, J. (1983) 'I am bad, no good, can't think', in Boston, M, and Szur, R., eds., *Psychotherapy with Severely Deprived Children*. London: Routledge.

Steiner, J. (1982) 'Perverse relationships between parts of the self: a clinical illustration', *International Journal of Psycho-Analysis*, 63: 241-251.

Steiner, J. (1987) 'The interplay between pathological organizations and the paranoid-schizoid and depressive positions', *International Journal of Psycho-Analysis*, 68: 69-80.

Steiner, J. (1993) *Psychic Retreats*. London: Routledge.

Symington, J. (1985) 'The survival function of primitive omnipotence', *International Journal of Psycho-Analysis*, 66: 481-486.

Waddell, M. and Williams, G. (1991) 'Reflections on Perverse States of Mind', in Free Associations, vol.2, part 1, no. 22: 203-213.

End Note

An earlier version of Chapter 1 appeared in 1982, *Eta evolutivo*, *13*, 17-27; of Chapter 2 in Boston, M. and Szur, R. eds (1983), *Psychotherapy with Severely Deprived Children*. London: Routledge & Keegan Paul; of Chapter 3 in 1974, *Journal of Child Psychotherapy*, *3*(4), 15-28; of Chapter 4 in Williams et al. ed. (1990) *Interazione terapeutico in contesti diversi: esperience e ricerche in psicoterapia infantile*. Napels: Instituto italiano per gli studi filosofici; of Chapter 5 in 1982, *Quaderni di psicoterapia infantile*, *9*, 69-86; of Chapter 6 in 1991, *Journal of Child Psychotherapy*, *17*(2), 3-4 and in Adamo, S.M.G. and Williams, G. eds (1991) *Working with Disruptive Adolescents*. Napels: Instituto italiano per gli studi filosofici; of Chapter 7 in 1983, *Prospettive psicoanalitici nel lavoro instituzionale*, *1*, 150-65 and in 1984, *Journal of Analytical Psychology*, *29*, 155-69; of Chapter 8 in Candelori, C. ed. (1996), *Dolore mentale e conoscenza*. Bologna: Cosmopoli; of Chapter 9 in Quagliata, E. ed. (1994), *Un buon incontro: la valutazione secondo il modello Tavistock*. Rome: Casa Editrice Astrolabio.

Index